AINSLEY HARRIOTT'S
GOURMET EXPRESS

Dorling  Kindersley

London, New York, Sydney, Dehli, Paris, Munich, and Johannesburg

Publisher: Sean Moore
Editorial director: LaVonne Carlson
Project editor: Barbara Minton
Editor: Tracy McCord
Art director: Dirk Kaufman
Art editor: Gus Yoo
Production editor: David Proffit

ISBN 0-7894-7499-9
First US edition published in 2000 by
Dorling Kindersley, Inc.
95 Madison Avenue
New York, New York 10016

This is a companion book to the PBS TV
television series Great Food presented by

thirteen
WNET NEW YORK

Sponsored by

www.looksmart.com

Produced by

●●●● west 175
productions   wine.com
The best of wine™

First published 2000 by BBCWorldwide Ltd
80 Wood Lane, London W12 OTT

Commissioning Editor: Nicky Copeland
Project Editor: Rachel Brown
Cover Art Director: Pene Parker
Book Art Director: Lisa Pettibone
Designer: John Calvert
Food stylist: Silvana Franco assisted by
   Sharon Hearne
Props stylist: Penny Markham

Recipes developed and written in
   association with Silvana Franco
Studio photographs by Gus Filgate © BBC
   Worldwide Ltd 2000
Location photography by Craig Easton
© BBC Worldwide Ltd 2000

Set in Eurostile and Humanist
Printed and bound by Butler & Tanner Ltd,
   Frome, Somerset
Color origination by Radstock
   Reproductions Ltd
Jacket printed by Lawrence Allen Ltd

All the spoon measurements in this book
   are level unless otherwise stated.
A tablespoon is 15 ml; a teaspoon is 5 ml.
Follow one set of measurements when
   preparing any of the recipes. Do not
   mix metric with imperial.
All eggs used in the recipes are medium
sized.

CONTENTS

INTRODUCTION

If you've had a hard day working at home looking after the kids or in the office, there's always another job that awaits you – cooking an evening meal.

For an instant quick fix, you could order a take-out, but these meals are often unappetizing, quite expensive, and not that nutritious. So before you pick up the phone, take a look at the wonderful recipes in *Gourmet Express*, which can be prepared in almost no time at all. The book is full of interesting, easy-to-make meals that have the right balance of color, texture, flavor, and great taste.

Fast food can often be disappointing, but many countries have wonderful street food. Inspired by those foods while on my traveling around the globe, I've developed a whole chapter of recipes for snacks and hand-held food. Just wait till you try my Celtic Samosas, NYC Foolproof Falafels, Shrimp and Prosciutto Pizzinis, Wrap and Roll Hot Dogs, and the new treat on the block – Nori-rolled Sushi.

If you're in the mood for soup, this book spoils you with choices. I've created some delightful, quick, and healthy soups for every occasion, plus some great appetizers that feed the eyes and satisfy the tastebuds.

But if you're up for doing a bit of preparation in advance, there's a whole feast of recipes that you can have ready to pop into the oven at a moment's notice for a delicious family supper. Try Super Shepherd's Pie, Ocean Cheese and Potato Pie, or Cheeky Chicken Tikka Masala?

There are lots more great chicken, fish, and meat dishes, and some really excellent vegetarian meals that will make you more than happy to try a meatless supper.

For those of you who sometimes get stuck thinking about what to serve with a main course, there's a chapter on side orders and hot breads that will give you plenty of mouth-watering ideas. And don't forget to dip into the sauces and relishes section for some interesting flourishes.

Finally, the chapter on sweet bites and drinks introduces you to new ways of satisfying your sweet tooth. Just try my terrific Portuguese Custard Tarts, Banana Splits with Warm Choco-fudge Sauce, or a Simple Saffron Kulfi – naughty but all very, very nice.

Food has never been more exciting or inspiring than it is today, and we can now get fresh produce from all over the world in our local supermarkets. Hooray! In *Gourmet Express* I've combined lots of those fresh ingredients with pantry essentials, an approach that fits in with the busy modern lifestyle. You'll be amazed at what you can whip together with a few potatoes, some bacon, and a can of crabmeat. Just a few tomatoes opens up all sorts of exciting culinary prospects, and with a package of pasta, some chorizo sausage, and a few Italian cheeses, Mediterranean food can come into your kitchen with little effort and loads of taste. So remember to stock up on those pantry goodies and you'll never be short of ideas at meal times – especially with *Gourmet Express* by your side.

Happy cooking!

Sage and onion bhajis

Genuine bhajis are made with gram flour, which is made from chick peas. I've decided to cheat a little by using regular white flour and getting the yellow color from turmeric. I've made them even British by adding the classic onion partner, sage, and it really tastes fantastic, especially with a dollop of Maddie's Mango Chutney (page 134) or Lovely Tomato Chutney (page 138).

PREPARATION: 10 minutes COOKING TIME: 5 minutes

SERVES 2

½ cup (50 g) self-rising flour

¼ teaspoon ground turmeric

½ red chili, finely chopped

10 sage leaves, shredded

¼ teaspoon salt

1 onion, sliced

vegetable oil, for frying

METHOD

1 Place the flour, turmeric, chili, sage, and salt in a bowl. Add enough water, about 5 tablespoons, to form a very thick batter. Stir in the onion.

2 Heat 2 inches (5 cm) of oil in a wok or deep frying pan and carefully drop the mixture into it using 2 tablespoons, 1 to scoop up the batter and the other to ease it into the oil. (You might have to try these in batches). Cook for 4–5 minutes, turning occasionally, until golden brown and cooked through. Drain on paper towels and serve warm.

Celtic samosas

Samosas are one of my all-time favorite snacks, especially straight from the pan. I vary the filling to match the vegetables but I have always got a few potatoes in the pantry and some peas in the freezer. My son, Jimmy, calls these "Celtic" samosas because they're green and white inside. They're fantastic with a spoonful of Maddie's Mango Chutney (page 134).

PREPARATION: 40 minutes + 30 minutes resting COOKING TIME: 10 minutes

SERVES 4

2¼ cups (250 g) all-purpose flour

2 teaspoons baking powder

½ teaspoon salt

large pinch ground turmeric

3 tablespoons (40 g) unsalted butter, chilled and diced

FOR THE FILLING

2 tablespoons vegetable oil

1 small onion, finely chopped

2 garlic cloves, finely chopped

1 red chili, seeded and finely chopped

3 medium (350 g) starchy potatoes, cubed and boiled

¾ cup (75 g) frozen peas, thawed

1 teaspoon ground cumin

salt

2 tablespoons chopped cilantro

vegetable oil, for deep-frying

METHOD

1 Sift the flour, baking powder, salt, and turmeric into a bowl. Using your fingers, rub the butter into the flour until the mixture resembles breadcrumbs. Stir in about ½ cup (150 ml) of water to make a soft dough. Knead well for a few minutes, then roll into 8 balls. Cover with a damp cloth and set aside for 30 minutes.

2 Heat the oil in a large frying pan and cook the onion, garlic, and chili for 3–4 minutes until softened and golden. Add the potatoes, using a fork to break them up. Add the peas, cumin, and salt to taste; remove from the heat and stir in the cilantro.

3 Heat about 2 inches (5 cm) of oil in a wok or deep frying pan. Meanwhile, roll out each piece of dough into a 4 inch (10 cm) round. Spoon an eighth of the potato mixture into the center of each round. Moisten the edge of each round with a little water, then fold over the dough to enclose the filling, pressing the edges to seal, then gently flatten out each samosa. Fry the samosas in batches for about 2 minutes, turning until crisp and golden brown. Drain on paper towels and eat warm.

Hot crispy
Cajun chicken sandwich

This is one of my favorite late-night snacks. I vary the ingredients, depending on what's in the refrigerator, but all you really need is half a chicken breast with the skin on and a couple of slices of bread, then make up the trimmings as you go along. Other good things to put in a hot chicken sandwich include sliced gherkins, grainy mustard, sweet chili sauce, sliced cheese, or cream cheese with a shake of Tabasco.

PREPARATION: 10 minutes COOKING TIME: 15 minutes

SERVES 1

1 boneless, skin-on chicken breast half

1 teaspoon Cajun seasoning, or ½ teaspoon Chinese five-spice powder and a pinch of cayenne pepper

salt and freshly ground black pepper

juice of ½ lemon (optional)

½ cup (50 g) mild blue cheese

1 tablespoon mayonnaise

4 cherry tomatoes, halved, or 1 small tomato, sliced

1 salad onion, sliced, or a few dice of raw onion

handful of salad greens, if available

2 slices of bread

METHOD

1 Season the chicken with, salt, your choice of spices, and pepper. Cook skin side down in a non-stick frying pan for 5 minutes so the skin is nicely brown and crispy, then turn and cook for about another 4 minutes until cooked through but still moist and juicy. Now squeeze over a little lemon juice over it.

2 While the chicken is cooking blend together the blue cheese and mayonnaise.

3 Layer the salad ingredients on top of one of the slices of bread and top with the moist chicken followed by the blue cheese mayo. Sandwich together with the remaining bread and eat warm.

TRY THIS: Use different types of bread – French bread or pita is equally delicious.

Hot crispy Cajun chicken sandwich

NYC foolproof falafel
with yogurt drizzle

Real falafel have to be made with dried chick peas because the texture of canned ones is too soft. I've cooked many versions in the past and this is an authentic recipe – just pop a few falafel into a warmed pita, top with a drizzle of yogurt dressing and a pickled chili and you'll get a snack that tastes every bit as good as one you'd buy on a New York street corner.

PREPARATION: 15 minutes + overnight soaking COOKING TIME: 15 minutes

SERVES 4–6 (makes 16 falafel)

1⅓ cups (225 g) dried chick peas, soaked overnight in water

1 teaspoon salt

1 teaspoon baking powder

1 teaspoon cumin seeds

1 teaspoon ground coriander

½ teaspoon cayenne pepper

1 garlic clove, crushed

2 tablespoons chopped fresh parsley

juice of ½ lemon

vegetable oil for frying

pita bread and plain yogurt, to serve

METHOD

1 Drain the chick peas and place in a food processor with the salt, baking powder, cumin, cilantro, cayenne, garlic, parsley, and lemon juice. Whizz until very finely chopped but not puréed. (If you have time, set the mixture aside for a couple of hours so that the flavors can mingle, but it's not essential.)

2 Heat 2 inches (5 cm) of oil in a deep frying pan or wok.

3 Using wet hands, shape the mixture into 16 balls, then flatten slightly into patties. Deep-fry in batches for about 4 minutes, turning occasionally until browned. Remove with a slotted spoon and drain on paper towels.

4 Serve 3 or 4 falafel inside a warm pita bread pocket, with a drizzle of yogurt over.

Olé nachos Mexicanos

This incredibly quick snack is easy to make at any time and especially good when my friends drop by.

PREPARATION: 5 minutes COOKING TIME: 5 minutes

SERVES 2

5 oz (150 g) bag tortilla chips

1¾ cups (200 g) canned chopped tomatoes

salt and freshly ground black pepper

4 scallions, thinly sliced

2 mild red chilies, thinly sliced

½ cup (50 g) Gruyère or Cheddar, grated

⅔ cup (150 g) carton sour cream

METHOD

1 Preheat the broiler to medium. Put the tortilla chips into a large ovenproof dish. Spoon the chopped tomatoes over them and season lightly. Scatter on the onions, chilies, and finally the cheese.

2 Place under the broiler for 5 minutes until the cheese starts to melt and bubble. Serve warm with the sour cream for a mouthwatering mouthful.

TRY THIS: Take a look at the wide selection of tortilla chips now available in your local supermarket. Choosing a variety such as the 'fiery hot' or 'cool sour cream' can really add an extra dimension to your nachos. And a sprinkling of pickled jalapeño chilies adds an authentic spicy bite to this great quick snack.

Shrimp tempura
and vegetable treat

Tempura is a Japanese dish of battered, deep-fried slices of vegetable and shrimp. There are lots of different ways of making tempura batter. I've simplified the process by dusting the vegetables with cornstarch before dipping them in frothy egg white – it gives a crisp, golden result.

PREPARATION: 20 minutes COOKING TIME: 15 minutes

SERVES 4

FOR THE DIPPING SAUCE

½ cup (100 ml) vegetable stock

4 tablespoons soy sauce

1 tablespoon sweet chili sauce

2 tablespoons dry sherry

1 inch (2.5 cm) ginger root, finely grated

sprigs of cilantro, to garnish

FOR THE TEMPURA

vegetable oil, for deep-frying

4 tablespoons cornstarch

½ teaspoon salt

3 large egg whites

1 lb 2 oz (500 g) mixed vegetables, e.g. whole baby spinach leaves, halved mushrooms, sliced sweet potato, squash, eggplant, red pepper

12 jumbo shrimp, peeled, tail section left intact

METHOD

1 To make the dipping sauce place the stock, soy sauce, chili sauce, sherry, and ginger in a large pan and bring to a boil. Simmer for 5 minutes.

2 Meanwhile, heat 1½ inches (4 cm) of oil in a wok. Mix together the cornstarch and salt. Whisk together the egg whites and 4 tablespoons of very cold water until light and frothy. Dust the vegetable pieces and shrimp with the cornstarch, then dip in the frothy egg; deep-fry in batches for 3–4 minutes until golden. Drain on paper towels.

3 Pour the sauce into small bowls. Pile the vegetables onto serving plates and serve immediately with the dipping sauce.

Tempura shrimp and vegetable treat

Hot-smoked salmon pâté
with toasted bagels

This is a twist on the classic New York smoked salmon and cream cheese bagel. Hot-smoked salmon is available from supermarkets and delicatessens and by mail order from various gourmet catalogs.

PREPARATION: 15 minutes COOKING TIME: 5 minutes

SERVES 4

1 tablespoon olive oil

4 scallions, thinly sliced

1 lb 2 oz (500 g) hot-smoked salmon, skinned and boned

8 oz (250 g) carton cream cheese

1 teaspoon creamed horseradish

dash of Tabasco

freshly ground black pepper

4 bagels

1 tablespoon of butter

METHOD

1 Heat the oil in a pan and sauté the scallions for 1 minute. Flake in the fish, then beat well, cooking for a further minute or two. Remove from the heat – if the mixture gets too hot, allow to cool slightly.

2 Add the cream cheese, horseradish, Tabasco, and black pepper, and mix together until well combined.

3 Split open the bagels and lightly toast. Butter generously and serve with the hot-smoked salmon pâté and, if you like, a sprinkling of thinly sliced scallions.

CHEF'S TIP: The hot-smoked salmon has a naturally salty flavor, so don't add extra.

Hot-smoked salmon pâté with toasted bagels

Webby cheese
and prosciutto flat bread

This is a wonderful casual snack that's quick and always impressive, especially with a bowl of black olives. I love to use Italian fontina cheese for this as it goes all gooey, webby, and stretchy as it melts. Other good cheeses to use are mozzarella, gruyère or even cheddar.

PREPARATION: 5 minutes COOKING TIME: 5 minutes

SERVES 1

1 teaspoon Dijon mustard

2 x 8 inch (20 cm) flour tortillas

1¼ cups (75 g) fontina, finely grated

2 slices prosciutto

freshly ground black pepper

1 teaspoon vegetable oil

METHOD

1 Spread the mustard on one of the tortillas and scatter on the grated cheese, ham, and plenty of black pepper. Place the second tortilla on top and press together firmly.

2 Brush a large non-stick frying pan with the oil. Cook the sandwich for a minute or so on each side until crisp and well browned and molten inside. Cut into wedges or squares and eat warm.

TRY THIS: If you fancy pushing the boat out, layer fresh basil or arugula in with the cheese and prosciutto.

Kofta rolls with chili-yogurt

These tasty little koftas are so much better than a lot of the kebabs you buy from fast food restaurants, they're much better for you too. The chili-yogurt has a wonderful fresh flavor and really sets the whole thing off with a bang.

PREPARATION: 15 minutes COOKING TIME: 15 minutes

SERVES 4

1 lb (450 g) ground lamb

1 small onion, finely chopped

1 tablespoon chopped fresh mint

1 tablespoon chopped fresh parsley

2 teaspoons chopped fresh rosemary

½ teaspoon each mixed spice, ground cilantro and ground cumin

salt and freshly ground black pepper

4 flour tortillas

1 red onion, thinly sliced into rings

FOR THE CHILI-YOGURT

1⅓ cups (300 g) yogurt

3 red chilies, seeded and finely chopped

2 tablespoons chopped cilantro

2 garlic cloves, crushed

juice of 1 lime

pinch of sugar

salt and freshly ground black pepper

METHOD

1 Preheat the broiler to high. Mix together the lamb, onion, herbs, and spices and season with salt and pepper. Divide the mixture into four parts and, using your fingers, squeeze it around skewers to form long sausage shapes.

2 Broil the kofta kebabs for 10–12 minutes, turning occasionally, until well browned but still a little pink in the center.

3 Make the dip: combine the yogurt, chilies, cilantro, garlic, lime juice, and sugar, and season to taste.

4 Briefly warm the tortillas for a few seconds on each side in a dry, non-stick frying pan, or for 10 seconds in a microwave, to make them soft and pliable. Place a kebab in the center of each tortilla, pulling it off the skewer. Scatter over the onion rings, drizzle over the chili-yogurt and serve.

Nori-rolled sushi
with soy dipping sauce

Sushi is high fashion at the moment; not only is it very healthy, but it tastes great too. I get asked loads of questions about it, so I've included this classic recipe that is delicious and not too challenging. You need a sushi-rolling mat to make this kind of sushi, and they can be bought cheaply at an Asian market.

PREPARATION: 30 minutes COOKING TIME: 15 minutes + cooling

SERVES 4

1 cup (200 g) Japanese rice

4 tablespoons white vinegar, such as rice vinegar or white wine vinegar

1 tablespoon sugar

1 teaspoon salt

½ cucumber, seeded

1 avocado

6 oz (175 g) fresh tuna or salmon

4 sheets nori seaweed

1 teaspoon wasabi paste (Japanese horseradish)

pickled ginger, to serve

Soy Dipping Sauces (page 142), to serve

METHOD

1 Begin by cooking the rice. Wash it well in warm water, then place in a pan. Cover with water so that it comes ¾ inch (2 cm) above the rice. Cover and cook gently for 12 minutes, or until the rice is tender and the water has been absorbed.

2 Meanwhile, mix together the vinegar, sugar, and salt and set aside to dissolve. As soon as the rice is cooked, stir the vinegar mixture into it and leave to cool completely.

3 Cut the cucumber, avocado and fish into strips.

4 Halve the nori sheets and place one half horizontally on the rolling mat. Spread 2–3 tablespoons of the rice mixture on the seaweed, leaving a ½ inch (1 cm) margin on the edge furthest from you.

5 Spread a tiny amount of the wasabi across the center of the rice, then place a row of cucumber and avocado or fish across the center. Roll up so the seam is on the bottom of the roll. Continue to make rolls, alternating the ingredients so that some contain just fish and others contain cucumber and avocado.

6 Trim the ends of the rolls with a sharp knife, then cut each into six pieces. Transfer to serving dishes and serve with a spoonful of pickled ginger and one of my Soy Dipping Sauces (page 142). They are simply delicious and heavenly healthy.

Nori-rolled sushi with soy dipping sauce

Wrap and roll hot dogs
with mustard onion relish

Serving good old hot dogs in a tortilla wrap brings them right back up to date, but you can always slip them into soft finger rolls if you prefer. So come on, wrap or roll, the choice is yours.

PREPARATION: 10 minutes COOKING TIME: 20 minutes

SERVES 4

4 jumbo pork sausages

2 tablespoons olive oil

1 large red onion, thinly sliced

1 garlic clove, finely chopped

1 teaspoon yellow mustard seeds

salt and freshly ground black pepper

4 flour tortillas

Maddie's Mango Chutney (page 134), to serve

METHOD

1 preheat the oven to 400°F/200°C. Place the sausages on a baking sheet and roast for about 20 minutes until cooked through and rich golden brown.

2 Meanwhile, heat the olive oil in a small frying pan and cook the onion and garlic over a low heat for 10 minutes or so until soft and golden. Add the mustard seeds and cook for another couple of minutes, then season to taste with salt and pepper.

3 Place the tortilla wraps in the warm oven for a couple of minutes to soften them up and make them easier to roll. Place a sausage in the center of each wrap and top with a spoonful of the chutney and the mustard onion relish. Roll up and serve warm.

Late-night egg and sausage-sizzle sarnie

When you're feeling hungry, day or night, the thought of a hot, juicy, eggy sandwich is enough to make the hair on the back of your neck stand up, (What hair, Ainsley?)

PREPARATION: 5 minutes COOKING TIME: 15 minutes

SERVES 1

2 teaspoons olive oil

1 pork sausage, cut into ½ inch (1 cm) pieces

2 scallions, thinly sliced

2 eggs

2 tablespoons milk

salt and freshly ground black pepper

2 slices white bread

small pat of butter at room temperature

1 tablespoon Lovely Tomato Chutney (page 138) or brown sauce

METHOD

1   Heat the oil in an 8 inch (20 cm) frying pan and cook the sausage for 5 minutes until golden. Add the scallions and cook for an additional minute or two.

2   Beat together the eggs, milk, and some seasoning and pour over the sausage. Cook for a couple of minutes on each side until set and golden.

3   Butter the slices of bread and slide the omelette on to the unbuttered side of one of the pieces of bread. Top with the remaining slice of bread, butter-side up.

4   Cook the sandwich in the pan for 2–3 minutes on each side until brown. Cut in half and eat warm with the chutney or sauce.

Harissa-rubbed lamb
in charred pita

I use lamb fillet for this dish because it's really tender. Alternately, you could use neck fillet which is cheaper, but a little fatty. Harissa goes fantastically well with lamb, but you could use also chili paste. I also find hummus a really good accompaniment to the lamb: you can buy it ready-made in supermarkets, or make your own using my recipe for Cilantro Hummus on page 33.

PREPARATION: 15 minutes COOKING TIME: 15 minutes

SERVES 4

1 tablespoon harissa or other chili paste or sauce

juice of 1 lemon

2 tablespoons chopped fresh mint

½ teaspoon sea salt

12 oz (350 g) lamb fillets

4 pita breads

1 bunch (50 g) fresh arugula

⅔ cup (170 g) carton fresh hummus or 1 recipe of Cilantro Hummus (page 33)

lemon wedges, to garnish

METHOD

1 Mix together the harissa, lemon juice, chopped mint, and sea salt. Add the lamb fillets, turning to coat in the mixture, and set aside to marinate for 10 minutes or so.

2 Preheat a broiler pan for 2–3 minutes. Add the lamb fillets and cook for 8–12 minutes until well browned but still a little pink in the center; remove from the heat and allow to rest for 5 minutes to tenderize the meat. Warm the pita in the same pan.

3 Cut the pitas in half and fill each pocket with the arugula leaves.

4 Diagonally slice the lamb into ½ inch (1 cm) thick slices and pack into the pita. Top with a dollop of hummus and serve warm with lemon wedges for squeezing over.

Coconut chicken satay
pockets

Chicken fillets are the little pieces underneath regular breasts. They are great for this dish because they're exactly the right size. Some larger supermarkets sell them in packages. If you can only get regular chicken breasts, cut them into ¾ inch (2 cm) wide strips, then hammer them out with a rolling pin to flatten them slightly. The result is delicious and exquisite.

PREPARATION: 15 minutes COOKING TIME: 10 minutes

SERVES 4

6 oz (200 g) carton coconut cream

4 tablespoons chunky peanut butter

2 tablespoons light soy sauce

1 tablespoon honey

few drops Tabasco sauce

¼ cup (25 g) dry roasted peanuts, roughly chopped

salt and freshly ground black pepper

9 oz (250 g) chicken fillets

4 mini naan breads, to serve

1 fresh lime, cut into wedges

METHOD

1 Preheat the broiler to high. Soak 4 bamboo skewers in hot water.

2 Place the coconut cream and peanut butter in a bowl and beat together until well blended. Stir in the light soy sauce, honey, Tabascos and peanuts, and season to taste. If the sauce is too thick, add a little water.

3 Pour the sauce into a shallow dish and add the chicken fillets, turning to coat them in the sauce. Thread on to the skewers and cook under the broiler for 4 minutes on each side until cooked through and well browned.

4 Warm the naan breads under the broiler, then split in half. Remove the chicken fillets from the skewers and push them into the naan breads. Squeeze over a little lime juice and enjoy

TRY THIS: If you want to serve the filled pockets with the remaining sauce, make sure you heat it thoroughly with a little water so you can drizzle it over the chicken.

Melting mushroom
Swiss burgers

For a truly sensational burger, jazz it up with a mouthwatering topping, such as the garlic mushrooms with melted Swiss cheese described here.

PREPARATION: 15 minutes COOKING TIME: 10 minutes

SERVES 4

1 lb 2 oz (500 g) lean ground beef

4 tablespoons chopped fresh parsley

1 egg yolk

salt and freshly ground black pepper

1 tablespoon sunflower oil

4 slices gruyère, emmenthal or other melty Swiss cheese

4 seeded burger buns and shredded lettuce, to serve

FOR THE GARLIC MUSHROOMS

2 tablespoons olive oil

2 garlic cloves, crushed

3 cups (250 g) chestnut mushrooms, sliced

½ teaspoon cayenne pepper

METHOD

1 Mix together the ground beef, parsley, egg yolk and plenty of salt, and pepper. Shape the mixture into 4 even-sized burgers.

2 Brush the burgers with the sunflower oil and cook in a frying pan for 3 minutes without turning.

3 Meanwhile, heat the olive oil in a separate frying pan and cook the garlic for 30 seconds. Add the mushrooms, cayenne and a little salt and cook for 2–3 minutes until softened and well browned.

4 Turn the burgers and lay a slice of Swiss cheese on top of each. Cook for a few more minutes until the burger is well browned but still a little pink in the center and the cheese is beginning to soften and melt.

5 Scatter shredded lettuce over the bottom of each burger bun and top each with a melted Swiss cheese burger. Spoon over the garlic mushrooms, place the lid on top and serve immediately.

TRY THIS: I make a classic burger like this with pure beef, but mixing a variety of ground meat can give you a really good result. Lamb is quite fatty but adds good flavor, so try half-and-half lamb and beef. Chicken and pork together and pork with sausage meat also combine to make great burgers, patties, and meatballs as well as fillings for pasta dishes such as ravioli or cannelloni. Also, you could try replacing the burger buns with English muffins for a change.

Parisian
mustard sausage rolls

Fresh croissant dough is available in the refrigerated sections of larger supermarkets. It's great rolled and cooked as per the package instructions, but even better filled with juicy sausages.

PREPARATION: 10 minutes COOKING TIME: 20 minutes

MAKES 6

1 tablespoon vegetable oil

6 pork sausages

1 x 8 oz (240 g) tube of chilled croissant dough

1 tablespoon Dijon mustard

1 egg yolk

pinch of salt

FOR THE DIP

4 tablespoons tomato ketchup

2 teaspoons horseradish sauce

METHOD

1 Heat the oil in a large frying pan and cook the sausages until nicely browned; allow to cool.

2 Preheat the oven to 400°F/200°C. Open out the dough, then break along the markings to give six triangles. Smear a little mustard into the center of each triangle, then place a sausage at the short, straight end and roll up toward the point.

3 Arrange the sausage rolls on a baking sheet. Beat together the egg yolk and salt and brush over the dough. Bake for 10–12 minutes until puffed and golden brown.

4 Meanwhile, mix together the ketchup and horseradish. Serve the sausage rolls warm with the dip.

Parisian mustard sausage rolls

Finger-lickin' chicken

Well, this is my simple but very tasty version of that famous take-out chicken dish. I actually find it a lot easier to use the oven, because you cook the whole lot in one go rather than frying it in batches. Once it's in the oven you can leave it alone – until it's time to serve it, that is.

PREPARATION: 10 minutes COOKING TIME: 40 minutes

SERVES 4

1 medium chicken cut into 8 pieces, or 8 chicken drumsticks and thighs

1 tablespoon vegetable oil

5 tablespoons all-purpose flour

1 tablespoon Cajun seasoning

1 teaspoon cayenne pepper

½ teaspoon salt

METHOD

1 Preheat the oven to 425°F/220°C. Rub the chicken skin with the oil. Place the flour, Cajun seasoning, cayenne pepper and salt in a large bowl and mix well together.

2 Toss the chicken pieces in the flour until lightly coated. Place the chicken on a wire rack and on top of a baking sheet. Cook the chicken for 35–45 minutes until well done with a good crispy skin; serve hot and eat with your fingers.

No-cook oh so spring rolls

I buy rice paper wrappers from my local Asian grocery. They're really cheap and the best thing about them is that you just need to soak them in hot water before using, although they need to be handled carefully to avoid tearing. Make sure you buy the savory variety rather than those used for cookies and sweets. These rolls are oh so scrummy.

PREPARATION: 20 minutes

SERVES 4

3 x 6 inch (7.5 x 15 cm) rice paper wrappers

1 carrot, cut into matchsticks

4 inch (10 cm) piece cucumber cut into matchsticks

4 scallions, shredded

1 teaspoon toasted sesame seeds

2 tablespoons hoisin sauce

12 oz (350 g) cooked chicken, shredded

METHOD

1 Place the rice paper wrappers in an ovenproof bowl and cover with hot water; leave to soak for 5 minutes until soft and pliable.

2 In a separate bowl, toss together the carrot, cucumber, scallions and sesame seeds.

3 Drain the rice papers on a clean dish towel and spread 1 teaspoon of hoisin sauce across the center of each. Pile the vegetables and then the chicken on top.

4 Fold two sides in, then roll up to make a neat cylindrical shape. Serve within an hour or two.

CHEF'S TIP: The spring rolls are not at their best if made up too far ahead of time. Instead, prepare the vegetables and the chicken, cover separately, and chill until ready to use.

Spiced, speckled
tuna mayonnaise on rye

There are lots of different rye breads available. Pumpernickel can be strongly flavored and crumbly, so I prefer to use a malted rye or a sourdough bread for this special sandwich. You can also serve these as open sandwiches – just garnish with a sprig of cilantro and serve with a few ripe cherry tomatoes and olives.

PREPARATION: 10 minutes

SERVES 1

1 small can of tuna in brine, drained

1 shallot, very finely chopped

1 garlic clove, crushed

3 tablespoons mayonnaise

pinch of cayenne pepper

2 tablespoons chopped cilantro

salt and freshly ground black pepper

small pat of butter, at room temperature

2 slices light rye bread

2 oz (50 g) bag handcooked salted potato chips

METHOD

1 Mix together the tuna, shallot, garlic, mayonnaise, cayenne, and cilantro and season to taste.

2 Butter the bread, then spread over the tuna mixture. Crumble the chips into small pieces and scatter over the tuna. Grind over a little black pepper, top with the remaining slice of bread. Cut in half and eat immediately.

Cilantro hummus
with crispy garlic pita

Hummus is wonderful spread on crackers or chunks of warm bread, or scooped up with toasted crispy garlic pita bread.

PREPARATION: 10 minutes COOKING TIME: 5 minutes

SERVES 6

2 garlic cloves, roughly chopped

2 mild red chilies, seeded and roughly chopped

large bunch cilantro, roughly chopped

2 x 15 oz (420 g) cans chick peas, drained

juice of 1 lime

4 tablespoons olive oil

salt and freshly ground black pepper

FOR THE CRISPY GARLIC PITA

3 tablespoons olive oil

2 garlic cloves, crushed

2 tablespoons chopped fresh parsley

4 white pita breads

METHOD

1 Place the garlic, chilies, and cilantro in a food processor and whizz until finely chopped. Add the chick peas and whizz until well blended.

2 With the motor running, squeeze in the lime juice and drizzle in the olive oil to make a fairly coarse paste. Season well to taste and spoon into a serving bowl.

3 Meanwhile, mix together the olive oil, garlic, and parsley and season. Heat one side of the pita breads under a hot broiler for about 1 minute until well browned.

4 Turn over the bread, then use a knife to slash the softer surface 4–5 times without cutting through the bread. Brush with the herb and oil mixture and return to the broiler until bubbling and toasted (about 1 minute).

5 When cool, break into pieces and serve with the yummy hummus.

CHEF'S TIP: This is one of my favorite picnic recipes. Spoon the hummus into a zip lock bag and pack the pita into an airtight box until you're ready to eat them. Don't forget to pack that crisp, chilled white wine.

Shrimp
and chili ginger cakes

These soft, fluffy fritters are delicious, especially when drizzled with my Sweet Chili Sauce (page 143) or a squeeze of fresh lime juice.

PREPARATION: 15 minutes COOKING TIME: 10 minutes

SERVES 4 (makes 12)

2 thick slices white bread, crusts removed, about 4 oz (100 g)

½ lb (250 g) peeled raw shrimp

1 green chili, finely chopped

1 inch (2.5 cm) piece fresh ginger root, finely chopped

4 garlic cloves, finely chopped

1 tablespoon chopped cilantro

1 teaspoon salt

1 egg

vegetable oil for shallow-frying

baby lettuce leaves, to serve

METHOD

1 Place the bread in a bowl, cover with water, soak for about 10 seconds, then squeeze out the excess water. Place the drained bread in a food processor with the shrimp, chili, ginger, garlic, cilantro, salt, and egg. Pulse until well blended.

2 Heat the oil and shallow-fry spoonfuls of the mixture for 2–3 minutes on each side until puffed and golden brown. Drain on paper towels and serve warm on a bed of baby lettuce leaves.

Shrimp and chili ginger cakes *with* Sweet chili sauce

Dimitri's festive feta triangles

This recipe brings back some wonderful memories of Greek holidays in Salonika – sunshine, sea, and my mate Dimitri. The quantities given here will make lots of triangles, so they're perfect for serving as a appetizer when friends come over, or just for family nibbles. They're also great for picnics, and they freeze beautifully, too (see TRY THIS below).

PREPARATION: 30 minutes COOKING TIME: 10 minutes

MAKES 16

2¼ cups (250 g) feta cheese, crumbled

6 sun-dried tomatoes in oil, drained and chopped

1 cup (150 g) pitted black olives (preferably Kalamata), chopped

4 tablespoons chopped fresh parsley

2 tablespoons chopped fresh sage

½ teaspoon coarsely ground black pepper

1 tablespoon olive oil

8 sheets filo pastry, roughly 7 x 12 inches (18 x 30 cm)

4 tablespoons (50 g) butter, melted

METHOD

1 preheat the oven to 425°F/220°C. Mix together the feta, sun-dried tomatoes, olives, parsley, sage, pepper and olive oil.

2 Cut each sheet of pastry in half lengthways to make long strips, roughly 3½ inches (9 cm) wide. Place a spoonful of the mixture at one end of each strip and fold the corner over diagonally. Fold over again to enclose the filling and continue down the strip to make a neat, triangular parcel.

3 Transfer to a baking sheet, brush with melted butter, and bake top rack of the oven for 8–10 minutes until golden brown. Serve warm.

TRY THIS: Arrange the cooked, cooled triangles on a tray and freeze them for a couple of hours. Wrap loosely in freezer wrap and pack into a rigid plastic box or freezer bag and return to the freezer for up to one month. Defrost thoroughly before cooking.

For a nutty alternative, sprinkle a few sesame seeds on top of the triangles before baking.

Char-broiled vegetables and hummus ciabatta

Broiling vegetables releases natural sugars, which gives them a lovely charred flavor. Place them between two pieces of sun-dried tomato ciabatta bread, add a spreading of hummus and a sprinkling of arugula or basil, and you really have a very exciting eating experience.

PREPARATION: 10 minutes   COOKING TIME: 15 minutes

SERVES 2

1 zucchini, sliced lengthways

1 red pepper, quartered lengthways and seeded

1 tablespoon olive oil

salt and freshly ground black pepper

1 ciabatta loaf

1 sun-dried tomato in oil, finely chopped

2 handfuls arugula or a few fresh basil leaves

4 tablespoons hummus

METHOD

1 Brush the zucchini and pepper pieces with oil, season and cook in a large frying pan for 5–6 minutes on each side until softened, browned and a little charred.

2 Cut the ciabatta into 2 equal pieces, then split each half open.

3 Sprinkle the bottom of each half with the sun-dried tomato and scatter over the arugula or basil.

4 Arrange the char-broiled vegetables on top, then spoon over the hummus on top. Place the lid of the bread on top to form a sandwich, cut it in half and serve immediately.

TRY THIS, Why not try broiling other vegetables, such as eggplant, leeks, asparagus or strips of carrot?

Tomato and
feta bruschetta

Serve this snack and take a quick trip round the Mediterranean – 'bruschetta' is the Italian word for toasted bread, while rubbing the garlic over the top is very Spanish, and I've added feta and tomato for a Greek touch.

PREPARATION: 15 minutes + resting time COOKING TIME: 5 minutes

SERVES 4

½ pint (250 g) pomodorino or cherry tomatoes

1¼ cups (200 g) feta cheese

small handful fresh mint leaves

small handful fresh basil

2–3 tablespoons olive oil

sea salt and freshly ground black pepper

1 ciabatta loaf

1 large garlic clove, unpeeled

METHOD

1 Place the tomatoes in a heavy bowl, then use the end of a rolling pin to mash them and roughly flatten them open.

2 Crumble or roughly dice the feta into the bowl. Roughly tear in the herbs, then add 2 tablespoons of olive oil and plenty of seasoning. Set aside for at least a couple of hours.

3 Split the ciabatta in half lengthwize, then cut each half crosswize into 4 roughly equal-sized pieces. Drizzle the cut sides with a little olive oil and heat under a preheated broiler until golden brown.

4 Cut the garlic clove in half and rub the cut sides over the surface of the toasted bread; sprinkle lightly with salt. Pile the tomato mixture on top and serve. A little extra coarsely ground black pepper gives the bruschetta the perfect finish.

Crispy crunchy
corn fritters

Memories of my childhood come flooding back when I think of these delightful fritters. My late mother, Peppy, would always make these for a weekend treat, accompanied with tomatoes and honey bacon. Mmmm…

PREPARATION: 5 minutes COOKING TIME: 10 minutes

SERVES 4

15 oz (420 g) can creamed corn

2 scallions, finely chopped

2 tablespoons chopped fresh parsley

4–5 heaped tablespoons cornstarch

salt and freshly ground black pepper

vegetable oil, for frying

sour cream, to serve

METHOD

1 Mix together the corn, onions, parsley, cornstarch, and plenty of seasoning.

2 Heat a little oil in a large frying pan and cook large spoonfuls of the mixture for 2–3 minutes on each side until crisp and golden. Drain on paper towels and serve with a dollop of sour cream and a little freshly ground black pepper.

TRY THIS: Why not broil some bacon until crisp and scatter on top of the sour cream?

Roasted tomato
and crème fraîche soup

Roasting the tomatoes intensifies their flavor – and it's still a very easy soup to make. I love to serve this with Mozzamary Garlic Bread (page 118).

PREPARATION: 30 minutes COOKING TIME: 45 minutes

SERVES 4

8 ripe tomatoes, halved

1 red onion, cut into quarters

1 head of garlic, halved horizontally

2 sprigs thyme

2 tablespoons olive oil

sea salt and freshly ground black pepper

3½ cups (1 liter) hot vegetable stock

½ cup (100 g) crème fraîche

3 tablespoons chopped fresh parsley

warm bread, to serve

METHOD

1 Preheat the oven to 400°F/200°C. Place the tomatoes, red onion, garlic, and thyme in a roasting pan and drizzle the olive oil over all. Season generously and roast for 30 minutes until softened and a little charred.

2 Remove the onions and garlic from the roasting pan and set aside. Pour half the stock over the tomatoes and return to the oven for 10 minutes.

3 Meanwhile, slip the onions and garlic out of their papery skins and whizz in a food processor to form a paste.

4 Remove the roasting pan from the oven, discard the thyme, then add the stock and tomatoes to the food processor, scraping up any residue with a wooden spoon.

5 Strain the mixture into a clean pan and add the remaining stock and the crème fraîche. Heat gently and season to taste. Stir in the parsley, ladle into bowls, and serve with warm crusty bread.

Roasted tomato and crème fraîche soup *with* Mozzamary garlic bread

Butternut squash spiced soup

If you have not tried squash, this is a great way to enjoy it. Squash cooks down to a smooth purée making a lovely rich soup. I like to make this with butternut squash, which has great flavor, but you can use other squashes, or another delicious substitute is pumpkin.

PREPARATION: 10 minutes COOKING TIME: 40 minutes

SERVES 4

1 tablespoon olive oil

1 onion, finely chopped

2 lb (1 kg) diced squash or pumpkin

1 teaspoon cumin seeds

3 tablespoons curry paste

3½ cups (1 liter) hot vegetable stock

1⅛ cups (275 ml) heavy cream

3 tablespoons chopped cilantro

juice of ½ lemon

salt and freshly ground black pepper

warm naan bread, to serve

extra cream for swirling (optional but nice)

METHOD

1 Heat the oil in a large pan and cook the onion and squash or pumpkin over a gentle heat for 5–8 minutes until beginning to turn golden. Add the cumin seeds and cook for an additional minute.

2 Stir in the curry paste, pour over the hot stock, cover and simmer for 30 minutes until tender.

3 Liquidize with a hand mixer or push the mixture through a sieve. Return to the pan, stir in the cream, and heat through gently. Stir in the cilantro and squeeze in the lemon juice. Season with salt and pepper to taste. Ladle into bowls and serve with warm naan bread.

Easy lentil supper soup

This delicious and substantial vegetarian soup is so easy and economical to make, and it's even better on day two. My late mother used to cook it slowly with a ham hock; so for you ham lovers, simply shred up some smoked ham or pancetta and add 5 minutes before serving.

PREPARATION: 10 minutes COOKING TIME: 35 minutes

SERVES 4

1 tablespoon olive oil

1 onion, finely chopped

2 carrots, finely diced

2 garlic cloves, finely chopped

1 red chili, seeded and finely diced

1 teaspoon yellow mustard seeds

3 tomatoes, roughly diced

½ cup (100 g) red lentils

4 cups (1.2 liters) vegetable stock

juice of ½ lemon

salt and freshly ground black pepper

METHOD

1 Heat the oil in a large pan and cook the onion and carrots for about 3–4 minutes until beginning to soften. Add the garlic, chili, and mustard seeds and cook for an additional couple of minutes.

2 Stir in the tomatoes, lentils, and stock and bring to a boil. Reduce the heat, cover, and simmer gently for 30 minutes until the lentils are tender and easy to crush.

3 Squeeze in the lemon juice, season with salt and pepper to taste. Ladle into warm bowls and serve.

Hot and sour
chicken and mushroom soup

Delicious hot and sour soups are all the rage at the moment. My recipe below is made with chicken, but you could also try making it with shrimp, diced or ground pork, or just extra vegetables. Look out for frozen wontons and fish wontons in Asian markets or good supermarkets – the wontons make a great addition to the soup. Or serve the soup with Sesame Shrimp Toasts (page 112).

PREPARATION: 10 minutes COOKING TIME: 15 minutes

SERVES 2

1 lemon grass stalk

2 cups (600 ml) hot chicken stock

4 boneless, skinless chicken thighs, diced

1–2 teaspoons Thai red curry paste

1 shallot, finely chopped

1½ cups (100 g) shiitake mushrooms, sliced, or canned straw mushrooms, halved

2 teaspoons dark brown sugar

2 teaspoons fish sauce

juice of 1 lemon

salt and freshly ground black pepper

1 scallion, thinly sliced

1 red chili, thinly sliced

handful of cilantro leaves

METHOD

1 Flatten the lemon grass stalk with a rolling pin or meat mallet and place in a pan with the chicken stock, chicken, curry paste, and shallot; bring to a boil.

2 Add the mushrooms to the pan and simmer gently for 8–10 minutes.

3 Stir the sugar and fish sauce into the soup and simmer for 3 minutes until the chicken is cooked. Squeeze in the lemon juice and season to taste.

4 Ladle the soup into bowls and scatter the scallion on top, chili and cilantro. Serve immediately.

TRY THIS: If any of my family are feeling a bit unwell, I throw lots of shredded ginger root into the broth for a really soothing soup – especially good for coughs and colds.

Curried mussel soup

No, really, try it – it's fantastic, especially with the Green Onion Chapatis (page 117) or Tabletop Naan with Spicy Fried Onions (page 116).

PREPARATION: 20 minutes COOKING TIME: 20 minutes

SERVES 4

pinch of saffron strands

1½ cups (450 ml) hot vegetable stock

4½ lb (2 kg) fresh, live mussels, cleaned

½ cup (150 ml) dry white wine

1 tablespoon of butter

1 shallot, finely chopped

2 garlic cloves, peeled and finely chopped

1 small hot chili, seeded and finely chopped

¾ inch (2 cm) piece fresh ginger, finely chopped

½ teaspoon ground turmeric

½ teaspoon garam masala

½ cup (150 ml) heavy cream

juice of ½ lime

salt and freshly ground black pepper

1 tablespoon chopped fresh dill

METHOD

1. Place the saffron in a ovenproof bowl and pour over the hot stock; set aside to infuse.

2. Place the mussels in a large pan and pour over the wine. Cover with a tight-fitting lid and cook for 5 minutes or so, shaking the pan occasionally until the shells open.

3. Strain the mussel liquid into a clean bowl.

4. Heat the butter in a large pan and gently cook the shallot, garlic, chili, and ginger until softened and golden. Add the spices, saffron stock, and mussel liquid and simmer gently for 10 minutes.

5. Shell the mussels, saving about 20 to garnish and discarding any that don't open.

6. Stir the mussels and cream into the pan, add a squeeze of lime juice, and season to taste. Warm through gently, stir in the dill, then ladle into bowls.

7. Divide the reserved mussels between the bowls and serve.

Rapido French onion soup and cheese croûtes

Simple but stylish, this version of the French classic is just right for a light lunch and takes minutes to make.

PREPARATION: 15 minutes COOKING TIME: 40 minutes

SERVES 2

4 tablespoons (50 g) butter

3 large Spanish onions, sliced

1 tablespoon sugar

2 garlic cloves, crushed

½ cup (150 ml) dry white wine

2 cups (600 ml) hot, fresh chicken or vegetable stock

1 tablespoon Worcestershire sauce

1 small baguette

4 oz (100 g) gruyère, finely grated

1 tablespoon brandy (optional but delicious)

salt and freshly ground black pepper

METHOD

1 Melt the butter in a large pan and add the sliced onions. Sprinkle in the sugar and cook over a high heat for 10–15 minutes, stirring frequently until you get a lovely caramel brown tinge to your onions. Add the garlic and cook for an additional 30 seconds.

2 Pour the wine into the pan and cook vigorously for 1–2 minutes. Stir in the hot stock and Worcestershire sauce, bring to a boil, reduce the heat, and simmer for 15–20 minutes until the onions are tender.

3 Preheat the broiler to high. Cut four diagonal slices of baguette and toast for 1–2 minutes on each side. Reduce the broiler heat to medium.

4 Pile the cheese on top of the toasts. Return to the broiler and cook until bubbling and golden.

5 If using the brandy, stir it into the soup, and season to taste. Then, using a slotted spoon, divide the onions between two soup bowls. Place the cheese croûtes on top of the onions, then ladle over the hot soup.

TRY THIS: There are lots of different ways to stop your eyes watering when chopping onions, for example, wearing glasses, chewing parsley, or chilling your onions before slicing them.

Rapido French onion soup and cheese croûtes

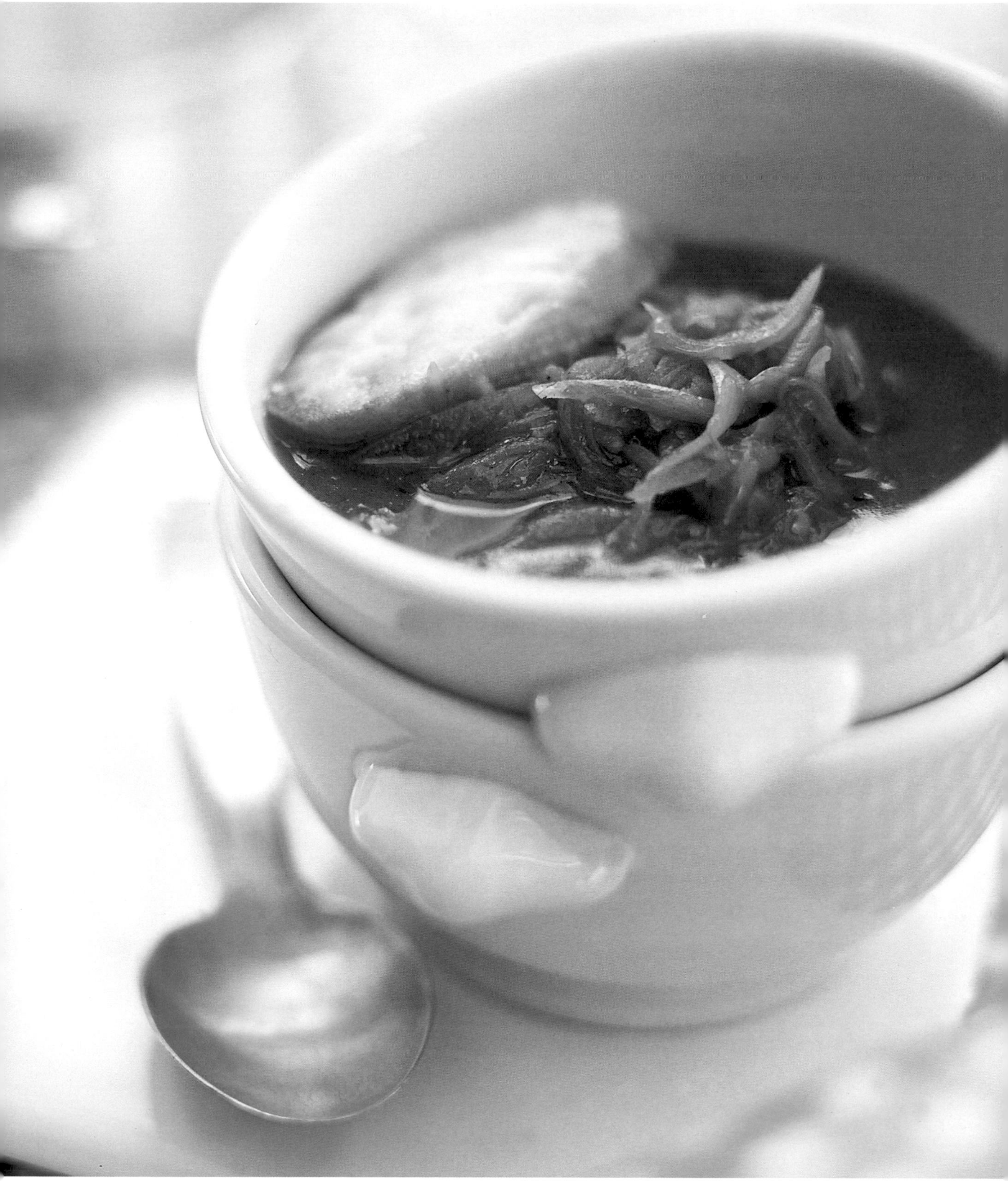

Succulent seafood
and roasted vegetable soup

This is a delicious, piquant soup full of flavor and packed with tender pieces of seafood. You'll need to use the oven and the stovetop, but the end result is well worth the effort. It's a great supper when paired with chunks of crusty bread.

PREPARATION: 15 minutes COOKING TIME: 50 minutes

SERVES 6

2 red peppers, seeded and quartered

1 eggplant, quartered

4 tablespoons olive oil

sea salt and freshly ground black pepper

1 large onion, chopped

2 celery stalks, chopped

4 garlic cloves, finely chopped

½ teaspoon chili powder

½ cup (50 g) all-purpose flour

4 cups (1.2 liters) hot fish stock

1 cup (300 ml) creamed tomatoes or tomato puree

2 sprigs fresh thyme

1 teaspoon sugar

9 oz (250 g) fillet haddock or cod, cut into 2.5 cm (1 inch) chunks

9 oz (250 g) raw shrimp

9 oz (250 g) squid rings

juice of 1 lime

2 tablespoons chopped fresh parsley

METHOD

1 preheat the oven to 400°F/200°C. Place the peppers and eggplant in a roasting pan. Sprinkle half the olive oil on top, season and roast for 25 minutes until tender and a little charred.

2 Heat the remaining oil in a large pan and cook the onion, celery and garlic for about 5 minutes. Add the chili and flour and cook for 1 minute, stirring constantly. Gradually add the stock, then the tomatoes.

3 Cut the peppers and eggplant into 1 inch (2.5 cm) chunks and add to the pan with the thyme and sugar. Bring to a boil, cover and simmer for 15 minutes.

4 Add the seafood to the pan and simmer for an additional 4–5 minutes until tender. Add lime juice, salt and pepper to taste. Stir in the parsley, ladle into bowls, and serve with crusty bread and chilled white wine.

Spinach, mint, and garlic soup

It may be simple, but this soup is really bursting with fresh flavor. I like to top it with crunchy pieces of fried bacon, but leave them out and you've got a vegetarian friendly bowlful.

PREPARATION: 15 minutes COOKING TIME: 30 minutes

SERVES 4

2 tablespoons olive oil

2 large white onions, roughly chopped

2 garlic cloves, roughly chopped

1 red chili, finely chopped

1 bunch fresh mint, roughly chopped

1 bunch fresh parsley or cilantro, roughly chopped

4 cups (1.2 liters) hot vegetable stock

3 oz (75 g) cubed bacon

1 lb 2 oz (500 g) fresh young spinach, roughly chopped

juice of 1–2 lemons

salt and freshly ground black pepper

METHOD

1 Heat the oil in a large pan and cook the onions, garlic, and chili for 10 minutes until softened and golden. Add the herbs and stock, bring to a boil, and simmer for 15 minutes.

2 Meanwhile, cook the bacon in a non-stick frying pan until crisp and nicely browned. Drain on paper towels.

3 Add the spinach to the onion mixture and cook for 2 minutes. Add lemon juice and salt and pepper to taste. Using a hand mixer, whizz the soup to a coarse purée. Ladle into bowls, scatter over the crispy bacon and a good grinding of black pepper, and serve with crusty bread.

CHEF'S TIP: Don't make this soup too far ahead of time – although it would still taste great, its lovely bright green color would begin to fade.

Newfoundland
crab chowder

If you've never made chowder, this is the perfect recipe to start with because it's so simple. The potato base makes it a truly hearty soup, so you could easily serve it as a casual main meal. Canned crab is a great addition to this dish, but I've also made it with cubes of smoked fish, such as haddock, or large, juicy shrimp. So go on, have a go – you won't be disappointed.

PREPARATION: 10 minutes COOKING TIME: 35 minutes

SERVES 4

2 tablespoons (25 g) butter

4 strips bacon, roughly chopped

2 shallots, finely chopped

2 large (450 g) starchy potatoes, diced

2 thyme sprigs

1 bay leaf

4 cups (1.2 liters) fish stock

2 x 6 oz (170 g) cans crabmeat, drained

¾ cup (200 g) crème fraîche

4 tablespoons chopped fresh parsley

salt and freshly ground black pepper

METHOD

1 Melt the butter in a large pan and cook the bacon, shallots, and potatoes for 4–5 minutes. Add the thyme, bay leaf, and fish stock, bring to a boil and simmer for 25–30 minutes.

2 Stir the crabmeat and crème fraîche into the pan and heat through gently. Stir in the parsley and season to taste. Ladle into bowls and serve.

TRY THIS: In Newfoundland they always crumble crackers into their chowder at the table, and I find this a really good way to serve it – just scrunch them in your hand and scatter over the top of your soup immediately before you eat it.

Pacific shrimp fu-yung

'Fu-yung' means a Chinese egg dish. Here, to go with the shrimp, I like to add a bit of shredded Chinese pork or sausage, or you can always throw in a bit of shredded ham if you like. Serve with a dollop of my Easy Mint Chutney (page 135) or Sweet Chili Sauce (page 143).

PREPARATION: 15 minutes COOKING TIME: 10 minutes

SERVES 4

6 eggs

½ cup (100 ml) chicken stock

2 tablespoons vegetable oil

4 scallions, thinly sliced

1 red chili, seeded and finely chopped

1 cup (75 g) shiitake mushrooms, thinly sliced

6 oz (175 g) cooked peeled shrimp

4 oz (100 g) pork or ham, shredded

¾ cup (75 g) bean sprouts

1 tablespoon soy sauce

handful of fresh cilantro leaves

METHOD

1 Beat together the eggs and stock until well blended.

2 Heat the oil in a large frying pan and stir-fry the scallions, chili, and mushrooms over a medium heat until beginning to soften.

3 Add the shrimp, pork or ham, and bean sprouts, cook for 30 seconds, then add the soy sauce and cilantro.

4 Pour over the beaten egg mixture and cook gently, stirring, until the egg is just set; serve immediately.

Deep-fried cod
in beer batter

Yes, this is a tasty batter to coat a piece of cod. It's the air bubbles in the beer that give the batter a good crunchy finish, so, unlike other batters, use this one as soon as it's ready. Try to choose a high-quality beer with a malty flavor for a really great batter. Deep-fry until crisp and golden, and serve with my Perfect Golden, Crispy French Fries (page 111) and (Minted Mashed Peas) (page 125) or Real Tartare Sauce (page 137).

PREPARATION: 5 minutes COOKING TIME: 20 minutes

SERVES 4

4 x 6 oz (175 g) pieces of cod

salt and freshly ground black pepper

1¾ cups (200 g) all-purpose flour, plus extra for dusting

½ teaspoon salt

1 egg, beaten

1⅓ cups (330 ml) bottle of beer

vegetable oil, for deep-frying

lemon wedges, to garnish

METHOD

1 Lightly season the fish and dust with flour.

2 Sift the flour and salt into a large bowl. Make a well in the center, crack in the egg, and gradually add the beer, stirring continuously, to make a smooth, frothy batter.

3 Dip the fish in the batter, making sure it is well covered, and shake off any excess. Deep-fry in hot oil for 4–5 minutes until crisp and golden. Drain on paper towels and serve hot, garnished with the lemon wedges.

TRY THIS: This quantity of batter is more than enough for four pieces of fish, so why not try dipping a few extras, such as red onion rings, to serve on the side?

Classic family fish cakes

These crispy fish cakes are a real family classic. I like to serve them with my Real Tartare Sauce (page 137) and a leafy salad such as the Arugula and Roasted Onion Salad (page 120), or push the boat out and go for (Perfect Golden, Crispy French Fries (page 111)) and (Minted Mashed Peas (page 125).)

PREPARATION: 25 minutes COOKING TIME: 15 minutes

SERVES 4

1 lb (450 g) starchy potatoes, cubed

1 lb (450 g) smoked haddock

1 hard-boiled egg, chopped

2 tablespoons snipped chives or chopped fresh parsley

salt and freshly ground black pepper

2 tablespoons seasoned flour

1 egg, beaten

1¾ cups (100 g) white breadcrumbs

vegetable oil, for stir frying

METHOD

1 Cook the potatoes in a pan of boiling, salted water until tender. Drain and mash well.

2 Meanwhile, place the fish in a sauté pan or frying pan and cover with boiling water. Bring to a boil and simmer for 5 minutes until just cooked.

3 Drain the fish and remove the skin. Using a fork, flake the fish, discarding any bones. Mix together the potatoes, fish, boiled egg, chives, and salt and pepper. Use your hands to shape the mixture into 4 or 8 even-sized round or triangular cakes.

4 Dust the fish cakes with the seasoned flour, dip in the beaten egg, then coat in the breadcrumbs, making sure they are completely covered.

5 Heat the oil in a frying pan and stir fry for 3–4 minutes on each side until crisp and golden. Serve warm.

Classic family fish cakes *with* Real tartare sauce

Golden crumb-crunch scampi

Scampi is actually the tail of the langoustine, which are often hard to find, and also expensive. I find it easier to use fresh shrimp – though if you can get hold of the real thing, do give it a go. Because of the lovely fresh taste of the shrimp, I prefer to keep this dish really simple and serve the scampi with a good dollop of my homemade Real Tartare Sauce (page 137) and a simple mixed salad made from lettuce, cucumber, and tomatoes.

PREPARATION: 10 minutes COOKING TIME: 10 minutes

SERVES 4

vegetable oil for deep-frying

32 large, raw shrimp, shelled

4 tablespoons seasoned flour

2 beaten eggs

1¼ cups (75 g) dried breadcrumbs

sea salt

lemon wedges and tartare sauce, to serve

METHOD

1 Heat about 2½ inches (6 cm) of vegetable oil in a wok or deep frying pan.

2 Toss the shrimp first in the seasoned flour, then the beaten egg. Give them a good shake to remove excess egg, then finally toss in the breadcrumbs. Deep-fry in batches for 2–3 minutes until golden brown and cooked through. Drain on paper towels and serve immediately.

TRY THIS: It's really important to use dried breadcrumbs for this dish as the crunchy coating is a lovely contrast to the juicy interior. I find supermarket breadcrumbs work very well, but if you have any stale white sliced bread, arrange it on a tray and let it dry out completely. Once hard and dry, whizz in a food processor to form fine crumbs, then store in an airtight jar until ready to use.

Ocean cheese and potato pie

This is a fabulous twist on a classic family dish. It's great for suppers after work because you can prepare the mashed potatoes and the fish filling the day before. When you're ready to eat, spoon the mashed potatoes over the fish mixture and pop it in the oven for 20 minutes. Sprinkle the cheese on top and finish it off as described in step 5 below.

PREPARATION: 15 minutes COOKING TIME: 20 minutes

SERVES 4

4 large (1 kg) starchy potatoes, cubed

2 cups (450 ml) milk

9 oz (250 g) smoked haddock

4 tablespoons (50 g) butter

¼ cup (25 g) all-purpose flour

1¾ cups (200 g) Cheddar, grated

4 tablespoons fromage frais

1¼ cups (150 g) frozen peas

7 oz (200 g) large, cooked, peeled shrimp

2 tablespoons snipped chives

salt and freshly ground black pepper

METHOD

1 Cook the potatoes in a large pan of boiling, salted water until tender.

2 Heat the milk in a frying pan, add the haddock and poach for 5 minutes or so until just cooked. Transfer the fish to a plate and let it cool. Do not discard the poaching milk.

3 Melt half the butter in a pan and stir in the flour. Cook gently for 1 minute, stirring continuously. Gradually add the reserved milk, stirring to make a smooth sauce. Bring to a boil, then remove from the heat and stir in three-quarters of the grated cheese, plus the fromage frais, peas, shrimp, and chives.

4 Flake in the fish, discarding the skin and any bones, and season to taste. Transfer to a ovenproof dish.

5 Pre-heat the broiler to medium. Drain the potatoes, mash well with the remaining butter, and season to taste. Spoon the mash over the fish mixture and scatter the reserved cheese on top. Grind over some black pepper, then cook under the broiler for 3–4 minutes until the top is golden. Serve warm.

Shrimp and peanut pan fried udon

Udon noodles are those lovely, thick white noodles. A lot of supermarkets stock fresh ones, which are vacuum packed, so they have a long shelf life. If you have trouble finding them, use regular Chinese-style egg noodles.

PREPARATION: 15 minutes COOKING TIME: 15 minutes

SERVES 4

11 oz (300 g) dried udon noodles or 1 lb 2 oz (500 g) fresh

vegetable oil, for frying

4 shallots, very finely sliced

2 large red chilies, seeded and thinly sliced

2 teaspoons sesame oil

11 oz (300 g) large, cooked, peeled shrimp

1¾ cups (200 g) fresh bean sprouts

handful of fresh cilantro leaves

2 fresh limes, cut into wedges, for serving

FOR THE PEANUT SAUCE

1¾ cups (200 g) salted roasted peanuts

2 garlic cloves, peeled

1 inch (2.5 cm) piece root ginger, peeled and roughly chopped

¾ cup (200 ml) carton coconut cream

1 tablespoon soy sauce

1 teaspoon hot chili sauce

METHOD

1 Plunge the noodles into a large pan of boiling water. Bring back to a boil, simmer for 1 minute until tender, then drain well. Cool under cold water.

2 Make the sauce: place the peanuts, garlic, and ginger in a food processor and whizz until finely chopped. Transfer to a bowl and stir in the coconut cream; add soy and chili sauces, to taste.

3 Heat ½ inch (1 cm) of vegetable oil in a wok or large frying pan. When the oil is very hot, add the shallots and chilies and cook for 3–4 minutes until crisp and golden brown. Drain on paper towels.

4 Pour most of the oil out of the wok, leaving just a thin coating, then add the sesame oil. Cook the noodles for 1–2 minutes., then stir in the shrimp and peanut sauce; stir in enough water (200–300 ml/7–10 fl oz) – to make a thick, glossy sauce and cook for 3–4 minutes until piping hot.

5 Stir in the bean sprouts and cilantro. Divide between plates and scatter the crispy shallot mixture on top. Serve with wedges of lime for squeezing on top.

Deviled, dusted whitebait

This is a traditional pub dish – truly delicious. Serve unadorned as an appetizer, or make it a main course by serving it with some lovely crusty bread and a crisp green salad – you can't go wrong.

PREPARATION: 5 minutes COOKING TIME: 5 minutes

SERVES 4

13 oz (375 g) whitebait, thawed if frozen

¼ cup (25 g) all-purpose flour

½ teaspoon salt

1 teaspoon mustard powder

½ teaspoon cayenne pepper, plus extra for dusting

½ teaspoon paprika

finely grated rind of 1 lemon

vegetable oil, for deep-frying

lemon wedges and herb sprigs, to serve

METHOD

1 Rinse the whitebait and pat dry with paper towels.

2 Place the flour, salt, mustard, cayenne, paprika, and lemon rind in a polyethylene bag. Add the whitebait and shake well to coat.

3 Deep-fry the whitebait in hot oil for 2 minutes until golden. Drain on paper towels. Transfer to a serving platter and dust with a little cayenne. Garnish with lemon wedges and herb sprigs and serve immediately.

Classic moules marinière

This French classic is really easy to make, and when mussels are in season – September to April – they're cheap and plentiful. Serve with salad, crusty bread, and a glass of your favorite chilled white wine – ooh la la!

PREPARATION: 10 minutes COOKING TIME: 15 minutes

SERVES 4

2 tablespoons (25 g) butter

1 onion, chopped

2 garlic cloves, finely chopped

½ cup (150 ml) dry white wine

½ cup (150 ml) fish stock

4½ lb (2 kg) live, clean mussels

3 tablespoons heavy cream

2 tablespoons chopped fresh parsley

salt and freshly ground black pepper

METHOD

1 Melt the butter in a large pan and cook the onion and garlic for 3–4 minutes until softened and golden. Then pour in the wine, bring to a boil and add the mussels.

2 Cover and cook over a high heat for 4–5 minutes until all the shells have opened. Transfer the mussels to a serving dish, discarding any that remain closed and leaving the juices behind.

3 Add the fish stock to the juices, bring to a boil, then reduce the heat. Stir the cream and parsley into the pan juices, add pepper and check for salt. Ladle the pan juices over the mussels and serve hot.

Roasted
lemon, bay, garlic cod

This is a really light dish – I've simply marinated the fish with a little garlic and parsley and cooked it over bay and lemon so it picks up the fragrance. Serve with a leafy salad or my New Millennium Posh Potato Salad (page 129) or (Mozzamary) Garlic Bread (page 118) and a good bottle of Chardonnay for a lovely lunch.

PREPARATION: 10 minutes + 10 minutes marinating COOKING TIME: 10 minutes

SERVES 4

4 garlic cloves, crushed

1 tablespoon chopped fresh parsley

2 tablespoons olive oil

salt and freshly ground black pepper

4 x 5 oz (150 g) cod fillets

2 lemons, thinly sliced

10 fresh bay leaves

METHOD

1 Preheat the oven to 425°F/220°C. Mix together the garlic, parsley, olive oil, and some salt and pepper. Rub the mixture over the fish fillets and set aside for 10 minutes or so.

2 Arrange the lemons and bay leaves on a baking sheet and place the cod fillets on top. Roast in the hot oven for 8–10 minutes until just cooked and a little charred. Serve immediately.

Roasted lemon bay garlic cod *with* Sweet potato and roast tomato cheese salad

Lobster
and papaya salad

Here's a touch of luxury when you're feeling well-off. Ask at your fishmarket to have the lobster halved and the meat removed for you – alternatively, you can buy lobster ready prepared in supermarkets. Serve with warm baby new potatoes in their skins for an exquisite main course, or how about my New Millennium Posh Potato Salad (page 129).

PREPARATION: 10 minutes

SERVES 2

2¼ lb (1 kg) lobster, cooked and shelled

4 cups (60 g) young salad greens

1 papaya, skinned, seeded and sliced

1 avocado, skinned, pitted and sliced

1 tablespoon raspberry vinegar

2 tablespoons olive oil

salt and freshly ground black pepper

chervil or dill sprigs, to garnish

METHOD

1 Cut the lobster meat into ¾ inch (2 cm) slices or chunks.

2 Divide the salad leaves between 2 large plates and arrange the papaya and avocado slices on top of the leaves. Add the lobster meat.

3 Whisk together the vinegar, olive oil, and some salt and pepper, then drizzle over the salad.

4 Garnish with herb sprigs and serve.

Crispy cache calamari

Memories of Mediterranean holidays come flooding back. There's nothing like a plateful of crispy calamari and a glass of dry white wine to make you enjoy the summer – also fantastic for a weekend lunch in the garden. I use a very simple egg-free batter for a really crisp result that's heavenly to eat. I only hope the sun shines! I like to serve the calamari tapas style, with Jacqueline's Potatoes Skins with Guacamole (page 106), a fresh tomato salad, and some juicy black olives.

PREPARATION: 10 minutes COOKING TIME: 10 minutes

SERVES 4

1½ cups (175 g) self-rising flour

1 teaspoon paprika, plus extra for dusting

½ teaspoon salt

1 lb (450 g) cleaned fresh squid cut into ½ inch (1 cm) wide rings

4 tablespoons seasoned flour, for dusting

vegetable oil, for deep-frying

cayenne pepper (optional) and lemon and lime wedges, to garnish

METHOD

1 Sift the flour, paprika, and salt into a bowl. Gradually beat in 8 fl oz (250 ml) water to make a smooth batter.

2 Dust the squid in the seasoned flour, then dip in the batter, shaking off any excess. Deep-fry for about 3–4 minutes until crisp and golden. Drain on paper towels.

3 Transfer the calamari to serving plates, dust with paprika or cayenne pepper, garnish with lemon and lime wedges, and serve.

TRY THIS: The body of the squid is just as tasty as the tentacles. Make sure the 'beak' has been removed (check at your fishmarket: if you can't find the 'beak', it's the hard, crusty bit directly above the tentacles), then batter and fry as for the rings above.

Tuna burgers
with red onion salsa

A great recipe for meaty fish, such as tuna. I've added wasabi, which is Japanese horseradish; it gives a fantastic kick to the fish, though you can add a dab of English mustard if you can't find wasabi. This stylish dish is a perfect appetizer for a dinner party, but makes a terrific main course supper if served with Grated Hash Browns (page 113) or chips (page 111).

PREPARATION: 25 minutes COOKING TIME: 10 minutes

SERVES 4

FOR THE SALSA

1 red onion, finely diced

2 plum tomatoes, seeded and finely chopped

1 green chili, seeded and finely chopped

juice of 1 lime

1 tablespoon olive oil

salt and freshly ground black pepper

FOR THE BURGERS

14 oz (400 g) fresh tuna

1–2 teaspoons wasabi paste

1 tablespoon sesame seeds

salt and freshly ground black pepper

1 tablespoon seasoned flour

vegetable oil, for stir frying

1 ciabatta loaf, sliced and toasted

METHOD

1 Begin by making the salsa: stir all the ingredients together, and set aside at room temperature for at least an hour.

2 Place the tuna in a food processor and pulse until coarsely ground. Mix with the wasabi paste, sesame seeds, and some salt and pepper. With damp hands, shape the mixture into 4 even-sized burgers.

3 Dust the burgers in the seasoned flour, shaking off any excess. stir fry for 2–4 minutes on each side until golden brown and just cooked through. Be careful not to overcook them or they'll quickly become dry.

4 Place the tuna burgers on the toasted ciabatta and top with a dollop of the salsa. Garnish with slices of fresh lime and serve warm.

Peppy's barbecue chicken
with Jamaican fried dumplings

The herby fried dumplings are the perfect accompaniment to my mum's spicy barbecue chicken. For an extra kick, why not add a ¼ teaspoon of chili flakes to the dumpling mixture and wash it down with a glass of my Sweet 'n' Easy Mango Lassi (page 166).

PREPARATION: 15 minutes + 20 minutes marinating COOKING TIME: 15 minutes

SERVES 4

4 tablespoons tomato ketchup

juice of 1 large lemon

2 tablespoons soy sauce

1 tablespoon dark brown sugar

½ teaspoon ground allspice (Jamaican pepper)

½ teaspoon cayenne pepper

½ teaspoon salt

4 skinless, boneless chicken breast halves

FOR THE FRIED DUMPLINGS

1¾ cups (200 g) all-purpose flour

1 teaspoon baking powder

2 tablespoons finely chopped parsley

½ teaspoon dried thyme

½ teaspoon salt

¾ cup (200 ml) milk

vegetable oil, for deep-frying

METHOD

1 In a large bowl, mix together the ketchup, lemon juice, soy sauce, sugar, allspice, cayenne, and salt. Add the chicken breasts, stirring to coat in the marinade, then cover and set aside for 20 minutes or so.

2 Meanwhile, make the dumplings: mix together the flour, baking powder, herbs, and salt. Beat in the milk to make a thick batter.

3 Heat 2 inches (5 cm) of oil in a wok or deep frying pan – the oil should be hot enough so that when a cube of bread is added to the pan; it browns in about 1½ minutes. Cook spoonfuls of the mixture, in batches, for 3–4 minutes until puffed, golden brown, and cooked through. Drain on paper towels.

4 Cook the chicken on a hot barbecue or in an oiled griddle pan for 8–10 minutes on each side until well browned and cooked through. Serve with mixed salad leaves drizzled with olive oil and lemon juice.

Charred chicken and pepper fajitas

The sight and sound of sizzling chicken and crispy vegetables arriving at your table is a joy to behold, and it doesn't have to be in a restaurant: this can be achieved at home for a fraction of the cost.

PREPARATION: 15 minutes COOKING TIME: 10 minutes

SERVES 2

2 large skinless, boneless chicken breast halves, cut into ½ inch (1 cm) wide strips

1 yellow pepper, cut lengthwise into 1 cm (½ inch) wide strips

1 red onion, thickly sliced

½ teaspoon dried oregano

¼ teaspoon crushed chilies

2 tablespoons vegetable oil

grated rind and juice of 1 lime

salt and freshly ground black pepper

4 x 8 inch (20 cm) flour tortillas

sunflower oil, for brushing

leafy salad, to serve

⅔ cup (150 ml) sour cream

METHOD

1 Place the chicken strips, pepper, red onion, oregano, chilies, oil, lime rind, and juice in a large bowl. Add plenty of seasoning and toss together until well mixed.

2 Heat a flat griddle or heavy non-stick frying pan. Add the chicken mixture and cook over a high heat for 6–8 minutes, turning once or twice, until the mixture is well browned, lightly charred and cooked through.

3 Brush the tortillas with sunflower oil and briefly warm them in the microwave for 10 seconds, or heat them in a dry frying pan for a few seconds on each side.

4 Serve separately, or pile the fajitas in the middle of your warm tortillas, add salad and a dollop of sour cream, roll up and enjoy. Serve with a bottle or two of chilled Mexican lager – *salud*!

Cheeky chicken tikka masala

Forget having to wait for your take-out chicken tikka: this is one of the easiest curries there is to make. If it's summer, why not have a go at cooking the chicken skewers over the old barbie?

PREPARATION: 20 minutes + 2 hours' marinating COOKING TIME: 25 minutes

SERVES 4

4 skinless, boneless chicken breast halves, cubed

1 inch (2.5 cm) piece root ginger, finely chopped

2 garlic cloves, finely chopped

1 teaspoon chili powder

salt and freshly ground black pepper

2 tablespoons chopped fresh cilantro

juice of 1 lime

2 tablespoons vegetable oil

1 onion, finely chopped

1 red chili, seeded and finely chopped

1 teaspoon ground turmeric

1⅛ cups (300 ml) heavy cream

juice of ½ lemon

Pulao Rice (page 122) or Tabletop Naan with Spicy Fried Onions (page 116),

to serve

handful of fresh cilantro leaves, to garnish

METHOD

1 Place the chicken breasts in a large bowl and mix with the ginger, garlic, chili, salt, pepper, cilantro, lime juice, and 1 tablespoon of the oil. Set aside for 2 hours.

2 Pre-heat the broiler to high. Thread the chicken on to skewers and cook under the broiler for 12 minutes or so, turning frequently until well browned.

3 Meanwhile, heat the remaining oil in a large pan and cook the onion and chili for 5–8 minutes until dark golden. Add the turmeric and cook for 30 seconds. Stir in the cream and cook gently for a couple of minutes.

4 Slide the chicken off the skewers and stir into the creamy sauce. Simmer for 5 minutes or so until the chicken is cooked through. Check the seasoning, adding some lemon juice to taste, and serve with rice or naan. Garnish with the cilantro.

Cheeky chicken tikka masala *with* Green onion chapatis

Wok-it chicken chow mein

If you've got some roast chicken left over from last night's dinner, simply shred it up and make this lovely chicken chow mein – perfect for a quick supper. An assortment of fresh stir-fry vegetables is great to have on stand-by for this.

PREPARATION: 10 minutes COOKING TIME: 15 minutes

SERVES 2

6 oz (175 g) egg noodles

1 tablespoon sunflower oil

1 onion, thinly sliced

2 garlic cloves, thinly sliced

½ inch (1 cm) piece root ginger, finely chopped (optional)

1 cup (100 g) bean sprouts

1 cup (100 g) snow peas, halved lengthwise, or peas

6 oz (175 g) cooked chicken, shredded

1 tablespoon soy sauce

1 tablespoon Sweet Chili Sauce (page 143)

METHOD

1 Cook the noodles in a large pan of boiling, salted water according to the packet instructions.

2 Meanwhile, heat the oil in a wok and stir-fry the onion over a high heat for 2–3 minutes until beginning to brown. Add the garlic, ginger (if using), bean sprouts, and snow peas or peas and stir-fry for 1 minute.

3 Drain the noodles well and add to the wok with the chicken and soy sauce; cook for 2 minutes until piping hot. Stir in the sweet chili sauce and serve immediately.

Scrunchy
sweet and sour chicken

Chicken and pineapple combine wonderfully, and this dish shows them to great effect. The dish has a lovely fresh flavor that's sure to be popular with all the family. I like to serve it with Excellent Egg and Ginger Fried Rice (page 110).

PREPARATION: 20 minutes COOKING TIME: 15 minutes

SERVES 4

2 egg yolks

2 tablespoons cornstarch

salt and freshly ground black pepper

4 skinless, boneless chicken breast halves, cubed

vegetable oil, for deep-frying

FOR THE SWEET AND SOUR SAUCE

1 onion, sliced

1 small red pepper, cut into 1 inch (2.5 cm) pieces

1 small orange pepper, cut into 1 inch (2.5 cm) pieces

1 lb (435 g) can pineapple cubes in natural juice

1 tablespoon cornstarch

2 tablespoons tomato ketchup

2 tablespoons light soy sauce

1 tablespoon white wine vinegar

handful of fresh cilantro leaves, to garnish

METHOD

1 Mix together the egg yolks with a tablespoon of water, the cornstarch, and some salt and pepper.

2 Heat 2 inches (5 cm) of oil in a wok or deep frying pan. Toss the chicken in the cornstarch mixture and deep-fry in batches for 5 minutes or so until crisp and golden. Drain on paper towels.

3 Empty the oil from the wok to leave a thin coating in the pan. Stir-fry the onion and peppers over a high heat for 2–3 minutes. Drain the pineapple cubes (reserving the juice), add to the pan, and cook for a minute or two.

4 Mix together the cornstarch and a little of the pineapple juice to form a paste, then stir in the remaining juice, the ketchup, soy sauce, vinegar, and ½ cup (135 ml) water. Pour this into the pan and bring to a boil, stirring until the mixture thickens.

5 Stir the chicken pieces into the pan and simmer for 5 minutes until cooked through. Check the seasoning, then divide between bowls, scatter the cilantro on top and serve.

Scrunchy sweet and sour chicken

Sticky maple syrup ribs

I love a 'sticky rib', and there's loads of different ways to marinate or glaze them. This is an easy and tasty way to get good results, and it works well on the barbie too. Go easy on the chili flakes if the kids are joining in. Try serving the ribs with Buttered Slam Baked Potatoes (page 102) and a side order of Citrus Couscous and Raisin Salad (page 130).

PREPARATION: 10 minutes COOKING TIME: 40 minutes

SERVES 4

2 tablespoons tomato purée

1 tablespoon cornstarch

juice of 2 limes

2 tablespoons maple syrup

2 garlic cloves, crushed

½ teaspoon dried chili flakes

½ teaspoon salt

1½ lb (750 g) pork ribs

METHOD

1 Mix together the tomato purée and cornstarch to make a paste. Stir in the lime juice, maple syrup, garlic, chili, and salt.

2 Pre-heat the broiler to medium. Rub the mixture into the pork ribs then arrange on a broiler rack. Cook under the broiler or on a barbecue for 30 minutes, turning occasionally, until well cooked and nicely browned. You can also cook them in the oven if you prefer: pre-heat the oven to 375°F/190°C, pop the ribs on a wire rack, place on a baking tray and cook for 35–45 minutes.

TRY THIS: This glaze is also very tasty on other cuts of pork, such as steaks or chops, but you will need to reduce the cooking time if the meat is boneless.

Crisp-crumbed
pan pork escalopes

This is a favorite dish in my house as it's lovely straight from the pan – especially when accompanied by some lovely Breaking Bubble and Savoy Squeak (page 107) and broiled tomatoes. Any left-overs are great the next day, sandwiched between a couple of slices of crusty white bread and topped with a squirt of mayonnaise or a dash of brown sauce – I'm salivating!

PREPARATION: 20 minutes COOKING TIME: 15 minutes

SERVES 4

1 lb 2 oz (500 g) pork fillet or boneless loin chops

2 garlic cloves, crushed

1 tablespoon Dijon mustard

¼ teaspoon cayenne pepper or chili powder

salt and freshly ground black pepper

2 cups (100 g) fresh white breadcrumbs

2 tablespoons freshly grated Parmesan

2 tablespoons seasoned flour

2 eggs, beaten

vegetable oil, for stir frying

lemon wedges, to serve

METHOD

1 If using pork fillet, cut into ¾ inch (2 cm) slices. Place a piece of sliced pork or a chop on a sheet of waxed paper or plastic wrap, cover with a second sheet and, using a rolling pin or meat mallet, flatten to a thickness of about ¼ inch (5 mm). Repeat for the remaining meat (or ask your butcher to do this for you).

2 Mix together the garlic, mustard, cayenne or chili powder, and a little salt and spread over the pork. Stir together the breadcrumbs and Parmesan.

3 Toss the pork in the seasoned flour, shaking off any excess, dip in the beaten egg and then into the cheesy breadcrumbs, to coat.

4 Heat the oil in a large frying pan and stir fry in batches for 3 minutes on each side until golden brown and cooked through. Drain on paper towels and serve warm.

TRY THIS: This method also works very well with frying steak, chicken, and turkey breasts.

Thai-style
yellow pork curry

If you like creamy, delicate curries, this is the one for you. To enhance the flavor, serve with plain boiled jasmine rice and a side order of Tabletop Naan (page 116) to help mop up all those lovely coconutty juices.

PREPARATION: 15 minutes COOKING TIME: 20 minutes

SERVES 4

2 tablespoons vegetable oil

2 scallions, thinly sliced

1 garlic clove, thinly sliced

1 lb 2 oz (500 g) pork fillet, cubed

1 eggplant, cubed

1¾ cups (400 ml) canned coconut milk

3 kaffir lime leaves, shredded

2 teaspoons yellow or green Thai curry paste

2 cups (150 g) shiitake mushrooms, sliced

1 cup (220 g) can sliced water chestnuts, drained

2 tablespoons light soy sauce

1 teaspoon fish sauce

handful fresh basil leaves

2 limes, cut into wedges

METHOD

1 Heat the oil in a large pan and cook the scallions and garlic for 2 minutes. Add the pork and eggplant and stir-fry for 3–4 minutes until the pork turns creamy white.

2 Stir in the coconut milk, lime leaves, and curry paste and simmer for 10 minutes.

3 Add the shiitake mushrooms and water chestnuts and cook for a further 5 minutes. Stir in the soy sauce, fish sauce, and fresh basil leaves. Serve with plain rice and lime wedges for squeezing on top.

Gina's classic super shepherd's pie

You've seen it before, but you really can't beat an old classic, and this is one of my family's favorites. What's different is the addition of soy sauce and Tabasco for a real kick that's guaranteed clean bowls. My neighbor Gina thinks it's *super*!

PREPARATION: 10 minutes   COOKING TIME: 25 minutes

SERVES 2

2 large (450 g) starchy potatoes, diced

1 tablespoon vegetable oil

1 large carrot, diced

1 small onion, finely chopped

11 oz (300 g) ground lamb

1 cup (300 ml) hot lamb stock

1 tablespoon brown sauce

2 teaspoons soy sauce

2 tablespoons milk

pat of butter

1 teaspoon cornstarch

¾ cup (75 g) frozen peas

salt and freshly ground black pepper

few drops of Tabasco

1 cup (100 g) grated cheddar – optional but nice

METHOD

1 Cook the potatoes in a large pan of boiling, salted water for 10–12 minutes until tender.

2 Meanwhile, heat the oil in a large frying pan and cook the carrot and onion for about 1 minute over medium–high heat, then add the ground lamb and stir-fry until well browned. Pour in the hot stock and stir in the brown sauce and soy sauce. Bring to a boil and simmer rapidly for 3–4 minutes.

3 Drain the potatoes well and return to the pan, mash well, then beat in the milk and butter until smooth and creamy.

4 Mix the cornstarch and a little water to a paste, and stir into the lamb mixture with the peas; bring back to a boil, stirring, until slightly thickened. Season with salt, pepper, and Tabasco, to taste.

5 Pre-heat the broiler to medium. Spoon the ground lamb mixture into a ovenproof dish and top with the mashed potato. Using a fork, mark a criss-cross pattern on the top and sprinkle the grated cheese on top. Place under the broiler for 3 minutes until the pie is speckled with brown or lovely and golden if using cheese.

Granny's corned-beef hash and fried egg

This is wonderful comfort food that I first tasted when it was cooked by the granny of one of my mates. Obviously, garlic and Tabasco have been added by me for one reason – *taste*. No wonder we covered the original in ketchup – sorry, Gran. Serve with greens or bok choi stir-fried in sesame oil, a splash of soy sauce, and a teaspoon of honey – yummy!

PREPARATION: 10 minutes COOKING TIME: 25 minutes

SERVES 2

2 large (350 g) starchy potatoes, peeled and diced

1–2 tablespoons vegetable oil

1 small onion, chopped

2 garlic cloves, crushed

7 oz (200 g) can corned beef

few shakes of Tabasco or other chili sauce

2 eggs

pat of butter

salt and freshly ground black pepper

METHOD

1 Cook the potatoes in a large pan of boiling, salted water for 10–12 minutes until tender.

2 Meanwhile, heat the oil in a small frying pan and cook the onion and garlic for about 5 minutes until softened.

3 Open the can of corned beef and turn out onto a chopping board. Chop roughly and add to the pan.

4 Drain the potatoes well and add to the corned beef mixture. Crush with a fork, stirring to combine the mixture. Cook for 5 minutes until a crust forms on the bottom. Add salt, pepper, and a shake of Tabasco then break up the mixture.

5 Add more oil if necessary and continue to cook the mixture until the base is golden and crusty. Break up once more and let it cook again until crusty underneath.

6 Meanwhile, heat a small frying pan, add the pat of butter. When it's beginning to melt and foam break in the eggs and cook, preferably sunny side up. Divide the hash between two plates, slide an egg on top of each and serve with a glass of iced lemon barley water.

Lightning lamb dhansak

One of the most popular dishes on any Indian menu and absolutely delicious. For complete authenticity, it can take a whole day to make lamb dhansak, but this lightning version combines all the flavors and tastes superb. Tamarind paste is available in large supermarkets or gourmet delis.

PREPARATION: 20 minutes COOKING TIME: 25 minutes

SERVES 4

1lb 2 oz (500 g) cubed lamb

2 tablespoons garam masala

2–3 tablespoons vegetable oil

2 onions, thinly sliced

2 garlic cloves, thinly sliced

7 oz (200 g) diced pumpkin or squash

½ cup (100 g) red lentils

2½ cups (600 ml) hot vegetable stock

1 tablespoon curry paste

1 tablespoon tamarind paste

2 tablespoons (25 g) sugar

salt and freshly ground black pepper

2 tablespoons chopped fresh mint or cilantro

juice of 1 lemon

Pulao Rice (page 122), to serve

METHOD

1 Toss the lamb in the garam masala. Heat 1 tablespoon of the oil in a large pan and quickly brown the lamb. Transfer to a plate and set aside.

2 Add a little more oil to the pan, then cook the onions, garlic, and pumpkin or squash for 5 minutes until softened and beginning to brown.

3 Now add the lentils, stock, curry paste, tamarind paste, and sugar and return the lamb to the pan. Bring to a boil, cover and simmer for 25–30 minutes, stirring occasionally, until the mixture is thickened and the ingredients are lovely and tender.

4 Check the seasoning, then stir in the mint or cilantro and lemon juice, to taste. Serve with pulao rice.

TRY THIS: Use the remaining squash (or pumpkin) to make the Butternut Squash Spiced Soup on page 44.

Lightning lamb dhansak *with* Pulao rice

Café chili beef tacos

This is a fantastic chili with a really developed flavor, which it gets from my secret ingredient – coffee! Try it, it really packs a punch. By serving with Buttered Baked Potatoes (page 102), you'll have a fast main meal to die for.

PREPARATION: 10 minutes COOKING TIME: 30 minutes

SERVES 4

1 tablespoon vegetable oil

1 onion, finely chopped

2 garlic cloves, finely chopped

2 red chilies, seeded and finely chopped

1 lb 2 oz (500 g) ground beef

1 teaspoon Chinese five-spice powder

14 oz (400 g) can kidney beans, drained

14 oz (400 g) can chopped tomatoes

½ cup (150 ml) strong black coffee

salt and freshly ground black pepper

8 taco shells

shredded lettuce plus sour cream and paprika, to serve

METHOD

1 Heat the oil in a large pan and cook the onion, garlic, and chilies for 3–4 minutes until beginning to soften. Add the ground beef and five-spice powder and cook for a further 3–4 minutes, stirring, until the meat begins to brown.

2 Add the kidney beans, tomatoes, and coffee. Bring to a boil and simmer for 20 minutes until the mixture is thick and fairly dark. Season to taste.

3 Fill the taco shells with shredded lettuce, then pile in the chili mixture. Top with a spoonful of sour cream and a shake of paprika and serve. A glass of chilled Mexican lager is always a winner with this recipe.

Pappardelle
with chili caper oil and baby mozzarella

For a light, versatile, and fun meal this is a real winner. The combination of wonderful strong flavors with the delicate taste and texture of mozzarella blends beautifully. Great as an appetizer for those impromptu suppers, or simply increase the quantities and serve as a main course. Strips of prosciutto draped on top would be a lovely addition.

PREPARATION: 15 minutes COOKING TIME: 10 minutes

SERVES 4

9 oz (250 g) pasta ribbons, such as pappardelle, fettuccine or lasagnette

3 tablespoons olive oil

large handful fresh basil leaves

2 garlic cloves, thinly sliced

1 red chili, thinly sliced

2 tablespoons pickled capers, well rinsed and dried

juice of 1 lime

sea salt and freshly ground black pepper

5 oz (150 g) boconccini (baby mozzarella), halved, or ball mozzarella, diced

METHOD

1 Cook the pasta in a large pan of boiling, salted water according to the packet instructions.

2 Two minutes before the pasta is ready, heat the oil in a frying pan and cook the basil, garlic, chili, and capers for 2 minutes. Squeeze in the lime juice and check the seasoning.

3 Drain the pasta well and return to the pan. Toss with the infused oil mixture and the mozzarella. Divide between 4 bowls and serve with a grinding of black pepper.

Deep-pan American-style
cheese-ring pizza crust

This is one of those thick pizzas that has the cheese inside the ring crust. It's a little more complicated than other pizzas, so if you don't want to bother making a cheese ring, simply scatter the cheese over the top.

PREPARATION: 25 minutes + 1 hour resting COOKING TIME: 20 minutes

SERVES 4

3 cups (350 g) strong white flour

1 teaspoon table salt

1 package instant yeast

2 tablespoons olive oil

1 cup (250 ml) warm water

FOR THE TOPPING AND CRUST

5 oz (150 g) ball mozzarella, drained

2 tablespoons chopped fresh parsley

1 garlic clove, crushed

salt and freshly ground black pepper

½ cup (100 ml) tomato sauce

2 tomatoes, thinly sliced

¼ lb (3 oz) thinly sliced pepperoni

4 green pickled chilies, sliced

METHOD

1 Place the flour, salt, and yeast in a mixer equipped with a dough hook. With the motor running, pour in the oil, and warm water and mix to form a soft, stretchy dough. Alternatively, make the dough by hand and knead on a floured board for 5 minutes.

2 Transfer the dough to a bowl, rub the surface with a little oil, and cover with a clean, damp dish towel. Set aside at room temperature for an hour or so until the dough has roughly doubled in size. Meanwhile, roughly chop the mozzarella and mix with the parsley, garlic and some seasoning.

3 Pre-heat the oven to 450°F/230°C. On a floured surface, roll the dough into a thin 16 inch (40 cm) circle. Arrange the cheese around the edge of the dough, leaving a 1½ inch (4 cm) border. Dampen the inner edge of the cheese ring, then pull the outer edge over to cover the cheese. Press down firmly to seal.

4 Carefully turn the pizza on to a large baking sheet so the joins are underneath. Spoon the tomato sauce within the border, then scatter the toppings on top. Bake for 12–15 minutes until browned and crisp. Cut into wedges and serve immediately with a lovely crisp, green salad sprinkled with olive oil and balsamic vinegar.

Shrimp and Prosciutto pizzinis

These delightful pizzinis are a great brunch treat, or are ideal as a light snack or appetizer. You could also serve them with Grated Hash Browns (page 113) for a tasty family dinner – the kids love 'em too.

PREPARATION: 15 minutes COOKING TIME: 35 minutes

SERVES 4

5 oz (150 g) package pizza-crust mix

1 tablespoon olive oil

flour, for kneading

FOR THE TOMATO SAUCE

2 medium (250 g) ripe tomatoes, seeded and roughly chopped

2 garlic cloves, finely chopped

4 thyme sprigs

1 tablespoon tomato purée

1 tablespoon olive oil

salt and freshly ground black pepper

FOR THE TOPPING

7 oz (200 g) large cooked peeled shrimp

4 slices prosciutto, halved lengthwise

handful of fresh basil leaves

fresh Parmesan, to serve

METHOD

1 Pre-heat the oven to 425°F/220°C. Place the pizza-crust mix in a large bowl and stir in the olive oil and enough warm water (about ½ cup/120 ml) to make a soft dough. Knead vigorously on a lightly floured surface for about 5 minutes until smooth and elastic.

2 Break the dough into 4 even pieces, then pat out between the hands to make rough 4½ inch (12 cm) circles. Transfer to a large baking sheet and set aside in a warm place for 10 minutes or so to rise.

3 Make the tomato sauce: place the tomatoes, garlic, thyme, tomato purée, and olive oil in a small pan. Simmer over a medium to high heat for 10–20 minutes, stirring occasionally until thickened and pulpy. Season to taste.

4 Spoon the sauce on to the dough circles, then scatter the shrimp on top. Place the strips of prosciutto across the top, then bake for 10 minutes until the pizza bases have risen and set. Slip the pizzinis off the baking sheet and continue to cook directly on the oven rack for a further 5 minutes until the bottoms are crisp and golden. Scatter a few basil leaves and some shavings of Parmesan over each pizzini and serve.

Tasty tuna pan fried pizza

This pizza dough requires no proofing, because I use a scone-style crust that you can fry in the pan. It's quick, simple and very tasty. Don't forget, anything goes, so just change the topping to suit what you have on hand.

PREPARATION: 15 minutes   COOKING TIME: 20 minutes

SERVES 2

FOR THE TOMATO SAUCE

1 tablespoon olive oil

2 garlic cloves, finely chopped

2 scallions, finely chopped

8 oz (200 g) can chopped tomatoes

handful of fresh basil, roughly torn

1 tablespoon tomato ketchup

salt and freshly ground black pepper

FOR THE TOPPING

6½ oz (200 g) can tuna in olive oil, drained and flaked into chunks

1 red onion, thinly sliced

¾ cup (75 g) black olives

3 oz (75 g) mozzarella or cheddar, diced

FOR THE DOUGH

2 cups (225 g) self-rising flour

pinch of salt

2 tablespoons freshly grated parmesan

⅔ cup (150 ml) warm water

2 tablespoons olive oil, plus extra for drizzling

METHOD

1   Heat the oil in a small pan and cook the garlic and onions for 2–3 minutes until softened. Stir in the tomatoes, basil, ketchup, and a little seasoning. Bring to a boil and simmer for 5–10 minutes until pulpy.

2   Sift the flour and salt into a large bowl, then stir in the cheese. Make a well in the center and pour in the water and 1 tablespoon of olive oil. Mix into a soft dough, then roll out into a 10 inch (25 cm) circle.

3   Heat 1 tablespoon of olive oil in a 10 inch (25 cm) skillet and cook the dough for 5–6 minutes until the underside is golden brown. While the dough is cooking, spoon over the tomato sauce and scatter over the topping ingredients. Drizzle over a little olive oil and place under a preheated broiler for 3–4 minutes until the top is golden and the base is cooked through. Cut into wedges and serve with lots of leafy salad.

Premier pistou-pasta

You know what it's like: home late from work and you'd love a delicious supper, well...a touch of French pistou blended with some al dente Italian pasta and you have the perfect answer on a plate that's refreshingly tasty and healthy. Some Arugula and Roast Onion Salad (page 120) served on the side would be a perfect addition.

PREPARATION: 10 minutes   COOKING TIME: 15 minutes

SERVES 4

11 oz (300 g) spaghetti or fettuccine

grated rind and juice of 1 lemon

small bunch of fresh flat-leaf parsley

1 tablespoon capers

½ cup (50 g) small, sweet black olives

a pinch of crushed chili flakes

4 tablespoons olive oil

1 large garlic clove

salt and freshly ground black pepper

Parmesan cheese, to serve

METHOD

1   Cook the pasta in a large pan of boiling, salted water according to packet instructions.

2   Meanwhile, put the rind and juice from the lemon into a large serving bowl. Roughly chop the parsley and capers and add to the bowl with the olives, chili flakes, and oil.

3   Crush in the garlic and season well.

4   Drain the pasta well and add to the bowl, tossing to mix. Shave or grate some parmesan on top and serve out at the table; remember to set out an extra side bowl for the olive pits.

Paper potato pizza

A potato pizza sounds a little strange, but wait until you try it – you'll discover how delicious it is. Cut into thin wedges and serve warm or cold with Arugula and Roast Onion Salad (page 120) – although, I've never had it cold 'cos there's never any left.

PREPARATION: 20 minutes COOKING TIME: 20 minutes

SERVES 4

5 oz (150 g) package pizza-crust mix

1 tablespoon olive oil

flour, for kneading

FOR THE TOPPING

9 oz (250 g) red-skinned or new potatoes

2 tablespoons olive oil, plus extra for drizzling

1 teaspoon fresh rosemary leaves

2 garlic cloves, crushed

sea salt and freshly ground black pepper

METHOD

1 Pre-heat the oven to 425°F/220°C. Place the pizza-crust mix in a large bowl and stir in the olive oil and enough warm water (about ½ cup/ 120 ml) to make a soft dough. Knead vigorously on a lightly floured surface for about 5 minutes until smooth and elastic.

2 Roll the dough out to make a thin 12 inch (30 cm) circle. Transfer to a large baking sheet and set aside in a warm place for 5 minutes or so to rise.

3 Meanwhile, thinly slice the potatoes using a mandoline, food processor or the side of a box grater. Toss with the oil, rosemary, garlic, and some salt and pepper.

4 Arrange the potato slices on the dough and bake for 10 minutes until risen and set. Slip off the baking sheet and continue to cook directly on the oven rack for a further 10 minutes until crisp and golden.

5 Drizzle over a little oil, scatter some sea salt on top and a good grinding of black pepper. Cut into thin wedges and serve.

TRY THIS: Scatter over some thinly sliced pancetta, diced smoked bacon, parmesan shavings, or arugula leaves.

Baked penne
with chorizo and Taleggio

Now this will tickle those taste buds! Baking pasta with cheese like this gives a really hearty, warming meal. Taleggio has a lovely flavor, but you could use camembert or port salut instead. I've added chorizo, the spicy Spanish sausage that's flavored with paprika: as it cooks, it releases its lovely juices into the dish. Absolutely scrumptious! Serve with a nice leafy salad drizzled with olive oil and splashed with your favorite balsamic vinegar.

PREPARATION: 15 minutes COOKING TIME: 15 minutes

SERVES 4

11 oz (300 g) penne

8 oz (250 g) carton mascarpone

2 teaspoons whole wheat mustard

4 scallions, thickly sliced

9 oz (250 g) chorizo sausage, cut into chunks

7 oz (200 g) diced taleggio cheese

salt and freshly ground black pepper

METHOD

1 Cook the pasta in a large pan of boiling, salted water according to the packet instructions.

2 Pre-heat the oven to 400°F/200°C. Drain the pasta well and return to the pan. Mix in the mascarpone and mustard, stirring until the mascarpone melts and coats the penne.

3 Stir in the scallions, chorizo, and cheese and season; then turn the mixture into an ovenproof dish. Bake for about 15–20 minutes until the top is crisp and golden brown.

Baked penne with chorizo and Taleggio

Buttered and slammed baked potatoes

It really is hard to beat baked potato skins when it comes to warming, nutritious, and economical food. They make great accompaniments to a main meal, and with a tasty filling are satisfying by themselves. Begin by choosing a good main-crop potato, such as a Russet, as they have a desirable starchy texture when baked. If you like a soft skin on your potato, rub a little olive oil into the surface before baking; if you prefer a crunchier skin, leave the potato in the oven for 20 minutes or so longer. For extra-quick skins, start in the microwave on high power for 8 minutes, then crisp up in a hot oven for 10–15 minutes.

You can bake new potatoes but you'll get a very different result because the flesh is firm and waxy. Rub baby new potatoes with oil and sprinkle with sea salt. Bake, then serve with, for example, my Lovely Tomato Chutney (page 138) or a cheesy fondue-style sauce for dipping into.

Whatever filling or topping I plan to serve my potatoes with, I always start with a tablespoon of butter and sprinkling of salt.

PREPARATION: 5 minutes COOKING TIME: 1½ hours

SERVES 1

1 large potato, weighing around 9 oz (250 g)

1 teaspoon olive oil

sea salt

small pat of butter

METHOD

1 Preheat the oven to 400°F/200°C. Scrub the potato and dry thoroughly. Prick in several places with a fork and rub in the olive oil; sprinkle lightly with sea salt. Bake for 1½ hours until the potato feels soft when gently squeezed.

2 Wrap the potato in a clean towel and slam it down onto a board; alternatively, place the potato on a serving plate with a dish towel on top and hit it with your fist. Both these slamming methods work really well because the force breaks up the potato into fluffy grains and usually causes a natural split.

3 Drop the butter into the split and sprinkle in a little more salt. Eat immediately or serve with your choice of topping: Here are some of my favorites:
• sour cream and chives
• tuna and garlic mayo
• cream cheese and smoked salmon
• curried baked beans with mature Cheddar
• sautéed leeks, cream cheese and black pepper

Eggplant chili jackets

My vegetarian friends simply love this recipe. It's quick, nutritious, and extremely satisfying. For a touch of class, I like to serve it with a dollop of sour cream.

PREPARATION: 15 minutes COOKING TIME: 25 minutes

SERVES 4

2 tablespoons olive oil

1 onion, roughly chopped

2 garlic cloves, roughly chopped

1 red chili, roughly chopped

2 large eggplants, cubed

2 teaspoons chopped fresh rosemary

½ cup (150 ml) red wine

14 oz (400 g) can chopped plum tomatoes

14 oz (400 g) can cannellini beans, drained

sea salt and freshly ground black pepper

4 baked potatoes (page 102)

METHOD

1 Heat the oil in a sauté pan and cook the onion, garlic, and chili for 2 minutes over a moderate heat. Add the eggplant and rosemary and continue to cook for a further 4–5 minutes until beginning to soften.

2 Pour in the wine and bring to a boil. Add the tomatoes and beans, season to taste, then cover and cook for 20–25 minutes or so, stirring from time to time.

3 Divide between hot, buttered baked potatoes and serve straight away.

Fluffed, puffed cheese
and honey ham baked potatoes

These baked potatoes are a big hit in my house, especially with the children.
The combination of honeyed ham and smoked mozzarella is absolutely delicious.
Needless to say, ketchup is never requested...

PREPARATION: 15 minutes COOKING TIME: 20 minutes

SERVES 4

4 baked potatoes (page 102)

1 tablespoon of butter

1 tablespoon Dijon mustard

2 eggs, separated

1 cup (100 g) smoked mozzarella, diced

3 oz (75 g) honey-roast ham, roughly chopped

3 tablespoons snipped fresh chives

salt and freshly ground black pepper

green-leaf salad, to serve

METHOD

1 After taking the cooked potatoes out of the oven, lower the
temperature to 350°F/180°C. Cut a ½ inch (1 cm) slice off the top of each
potato and scoop out the flesh to leave a ¼ inch (5 mm) thick shell.

2 Mash the flesh, with the butter, mustard, and egg yolks. Stir in the
cheese, ham, chives, and some salt and pepper.

3 Whisk the egg whites until fairly stiff and fold into the potato mixture.
Pile back into the shells and bake for 20 minutes until puffed and lightly
browned. Serve hot with a crisp green leafy salad.

Fluffed, puffed cheese and honey ham jackets

Jacqueline's potato skins
with guacamole

Crispy skins like these make really great party food, as well as an appetizing side dish. Serve them with a bowl of guacamole and the sour cream dip from my Baconeese Cream Potato Wedges on page 108. The potato flesh can be saved and used to make my delicious Grated Hash Browns (page 113) for breakfast or brunch the next day. My sister Jacqueline likes to add a portion of the potato to her guacamole. It really works a treat, but you must mix it in well – ideally, using a food processor.

PREPARATION: 15 minutes COOKING TIME: 20 minutes

SERVES 2

2 baked potatoes (page 102)

2 tablespoons olive oil

coarse sea salt

FOR THE GUACAMOLE

1 large, ripe avocado, halved and stoned

1 garlic clove, crushed

1 red chili, seeded and finely chopped

2 tablespoons chopped cilantro

juice of 1 lime

salt and freshly ground black pepper

METHOD

1 Bake the potatoes as described on page 102. Raise the oven temperature to 425°F/220°C. Halve the potatoes and scoop out the flesh to leave a ¼ inch (5 mm) thick shell. Cut each half into 3–4 strips, place in a bowl and toss with the oil.

2 Arrange the strips, skin-side down, on a sturdy baking sheet. Sprinkle with coarse sea salt and bake for 20 minutes or so until the strips are crisp and golden brown.

3 Next, make the guacamole: place the avocado flesh in a bowl and mash with a fork until fairly smooth. Stir in the garlic, chili, and cilantro.

4 Add lime juice and salt and pepper to taste. Transfer to a bowl and serve with the crispy skins.

CHEF'S TIP: If you have any guacamole left over, squeeze fresh lemon or lime juice over it, and cover with plastic wrap to help prevent discoloration.

Breaking bubble and Savoy squeak

Like Granny's Corned Beef Hash and Fried Egg on page 85, this is also a quick, throw-it-together dish. It's great on its own with a steak or fried egg, but best of all, throw in some crispy bacon or diced spicy chorizo for a supper treat in front of the tube.

PREPARATION: 15 minutes COOKING TIME: 20 minutes

SERVES 2

1⅓ cups (350 g) starchy potatoes, diced

half a small Savoy cabbage, shredded

2 tablespoons vegetable oil

1 small onion, chopped

2 garlic cloves, crushed

2 red chilies, thinly sliced

2 teaspoons Worcestershire or soy sauce

salt and freshly ground black pepper

METHOD

1 Cook the potatoes in a large pan of boiling, salted water for 8 minutes. Add the cabbage and cook for a further 3–4 minutes until tender.

2 Meanwhile, heat the oil in a large frying pan and cook the onion, garlic and chilies for 5 minutes until golden.

3 Drain the potatoes and cabbage well and add to the frying pan. Crush with a wooden spoon, then leave the mixture to cook over a medium heat for 2–3 minutes until a crust forms on the bottom.

4 Break up the mixture, stir in the Worcestershire or soy sauce and season, then leave to cook again until a crust forms on the bottom; break up again and cook for a third time. Spoon on to plates and serve.

CHEF'S TIP: Leave out the chili if you're feeding this to kids.

Baconeese
cream potato wedges

The combination of bacon, cheese, and potato is perfect. Add a chopped salad onion and sour cream and you're in heaven. I like to serve these wedges on the side with – and I know it sounds odd – the Classic Moules Marinière on page 65; they really taste fabulous. Of course, you can serve them with all sorts of other things, or on their own for a tasty snack.

PREPARATION: 15 minutes COOKING TIME: 40 minutes

SERVES 4

4 large (4 x 250 g) baking potatoes

2 tablespoons olive oil

1 teaspoon paprika

½ teaspoon sea salt

½ cup (75 g) bacon, chopped

1 cup (100 g) Gruyère or Cheddar, finely grated

4 scallions, chopped

FOR THE DIP

1 cup (300 ml) sour cream

4 scallions, finely chopped

1 teaspoon horseradish sauce

METHOD

1 Preheat the oven to 425°F/220°C. Cut each potato into 8 wedges and place in a bowl with the oil, paprika, and salt. Toss well together, arrange on a sturdy baking sheet and cook for 20 minutes, turning occasionally. Scatter over the bacon and return to the oven for 10 minutes until the potatoes are cooked through and golden and the bacon is sizzling and crispy.

2 Scatter over the grated cheese and scallions and return to the oven for a further 10 minutes until the cheese is melted and bubbly and the wedges are nicely browned.

3 Meanwhile, make the dip by stirring together the sour cream, scallions, and horseradish sauce. Spoon into a serving bowl, place the bowl into the center of a large plate, and arrange the cheesy wedges around the dip, scraping any cheese and bacon pieces on top of the wedges. Serve hot.

TRY THIS: If you have any left-over boiled or baked potatoes, cut them roughly into cubes and toss with the oil and paprika as before. Scatter with bacon and cook for 10 minutes, followed by the cheese for another 10 minutes. Hey presto, a scrumptious hash – great with a fried egg on top!

Baconeese cream potato wedges

Excellent egg and ginger fried rice

The secret to successful egg fried rice is to cook the eggs before you add the rice – it works a treat. With a touch more onion and ginger, this rice really titillates those taste buds.

PREPARATION: 5 minutes COOKING TIME: 10 minutes

SERVES 2

1 tablespoon vegetable oil

4 scallions, thinly sliced

1 garlic clove, finely chopped

¾ inch (2 cm) piece fresh ginger, grated or finely chopped

1 egg

1 cup (175 g) cooked long-grain rice

½ cup (50 g) frozen peas

1 tablespoon soy sauce

freshly ground black pepper

METHOD

1 Heat the oil in a wok and cook the scallions, garlic and ginger for 2 minutes. Crack in the egg and scramble with a chopstick for a couple of minutes until just set.

2 Stir in the rice and peas and continue to cook for a further 3–4 minutes until piping hot. Season with soy sauce and a few twists of black pepper and serve.

CHEF'S TIP: If I don't have any left-over cooked rice on hand, I use frozen rice. It comes in free-flow bags and works brilliantly in stir-fries and other quick dishes.Buy it at your freezer store or supermarket.

Perfect golden, crispy chips

People often ask me how to make the perfect fries that are crunchy on the outside and fluffy in the center. Well, here you have it and you don't even need an electric fryer. Remember to do the bread test for perfect results.

PREPARATION: 5 minutes COOKING TIME: 10 minutes

SERVES 1

1 large potato

vegetable oil, for frying

cubes of bread, to test oil temperature

salt

METHOD

1 Scrub the potato in clean, cold water and cut into fingers as thick or thin as you choose. Wash well to rinse off the excess starch and help prevent them sticking together during cooking. Dry thoroughly with paper towels.

2 Heat 2 inches (5 cm) vegetable oil in a small, deep frying pan. Test the oil temperature with a cube of bread – it should take 60 seconds to turn brown. When the oil has reached the right temperature – do not let it get too hot – cook the fries for 5 minutes or until pale golden.

3 Remove with a slotted spoon and drain on paper towels. Raise the heat slightly and, when the oil is hot enough to brown a cube of bread in 30 seconds, return the fries to the pan for 1–2 minutes until crisp and golden. Drain on paper towels, sprinkle with salt, splash with malt vinegar and eat immediately.

Sesame shrimp toasts

Once you've tried these toasties, you'll be making them again and again – they're so easy to do. Great with my Hot and Sour Chicken and Mushroom Soup (page 46), they also make a fantastic, very attractive, and quick snack. Now that's what I call impressive!

PREPARATION: 10 minutes COOKING TIME: 5 minutes

SERVES 4

6 oz (175 g) cooked peeled shrimp

¾ inch (2 cm) piece fresh ginger root, grated

1 garlic clove, finely chopped

1 egg white

2 teaspoons cornstarch

¼ teaspoon Chinese five-spice powder

¼ teaspoon salt

4 thin slices of bread, crusts removed

2 tablespoons sesame seeds

vegetable oil for shallow-frying

METHOD

1 Place the shrimp, ginger and garlic in a mini chopper or food processor and whizz until finely ground.

2 Whisk the egg white until frothy, then stir in the shrimp mixture, cornstarch, Chinese five-spice powder and salt until well blended.

3 Spread the mixture evenly on to the bread, then sprinkle the sesame seeds on top, pressing them in firmly with the fingertips. Cut each slice into 4 squares, fingers or triangles.

4 Heat about 3–4 tablespoons of oil in a frying pan; when hot, reduce the heat before adding the toasts. Cook shrimp side down for 2–3 minutes until golden, then turn and cook the other side – you might need a little more oil. Drain on paper towels and serve warm.

Grate hash browns

For a tasty treat, these hash browns are a perfect snack on their own. But I often make them for a weekend brunch served with my favorite sausages and cheesy baked beans.

PREPARATION: 5 minutes COOKING TIME: 25 minutes

SERVES 2

2 small, starchy potatoes

salt and freshly ground black pepper

vegetable oil, for frying

METHOD

1 Cook the whole potatoes in a pan of boiling, salted water for 15 minutes until just tender. Drain and cool slightly.

2 Coarsely grate the potatoes into a bowl and season generously. Firmly shape the mixture into 4 oval patties by patting the mixture together with the palms of your hands.

3 Heat a little oil in a large frying pan and cook the hash browns for 3–4 minutes on each side until crisp and golden. Drain on paper towels and serve hot.

TRY THIS: Add a nice touch of green with a few fresh chopped herbs – my favorite is thyme.

Garlic and parsley frittata

A frittata is simply an Italian omelette that you can add all sorts of ingredients to. It has a great taste with a lovely springy texture courtesy of the bread. A slice of white bread will do, but you could be more adventurous. Serve with a watercress salad.

PREPARATION: 10 minutes COOKING TIME: 10 minutes

SERVES 1

2 tablespoons milk

2 eggs

1 tablespoon chopped fresh parsley

1 garlic clove, crushed

pinch of dried chili flakes (optional)

1 slice white bread, torn into small pieces

sea salt and freshly ground black pepper

1 tablespoon olive oil

1 tablespoon freshly grated Parmesan

watercress salad, to serve

METHOD

1 Beat together the milk, eggs, parsley, garlic, and chili flakes, if using. Add the torn bread and some salt and pepper; set aside for 5 minutes so that the bread completely softens into the mixture.

2 Heat the oil in an 8 inch (20 cm) frying pan and pour in the egg mixture. Cook for 3 minutes or so until golden and almost set.

3 Slide the frittata on to a plate, then turn the pan over on top of the plate and carefully flip over so you can cook the other side. Scatter over the parmesan. Cook for a further couple of minutes until the underside is golden, the cheese has melted and the frittata is cooked through. Serve with a fresh, crisp watercress salad and a glass of your favorite Chianti.

Tabletop naan
with spicy fried onions

I've often eaten this in Indian restaurants, and it's always so yummy, with a great taste and texture. I've put together a recipe for making it yourself and it's certainly worth the effort.

PREPARATION: 30 minutes COOKING TIME: 25 minutes

SERVES 2

4 cups (450 g) all-purpose flour

pinch of salt

½ teaspoon baking powder

¼ teaspoon baking soda

1 teaspoon sugar

1 egg

⅝ cup (150 g) plain yogurt

4 tablespoons milk

2 tablespoons vegetable oil

2 tablespoons (25 g) butter, melted

FOR THE SPICY ONIONS

2 tablespoons vegetable oil

2 onions, thinly sliced

2 teaspoons garam masala

½ teaspoon sugar

½ teaspoon table salt

METHOD

1 Preheat the oven to 425°F/220°C. Sift the flour, salt, baking powder, and baking soda into a bowl. Stir in the sugar.

2 In a separate bowl, whisk together the egg, yogurt, milk, and oil. Pour into the flour mixture and bring together to make a soft dough. Knead briefly, cover with oiled plastic wrap and set aside for 15 minutes.

3 For the spicy onions, heat the oil in a pan and cook the onions with the garam masala, sugar, and salt for 15 minutes until golden brown.

4 Roll the dough out into a large rectangle. Using your fingers, press the dough into a jelly roll pan. Scatter over the spicy onions, pressing them into the surface of the dough with the back of a spoon. Bake for 10 minutes until puffed and browned. Remove, brush with the melted butter and serve warm.

Green onion chapatis

I find chapatis really useful. They're easy to make and you can add all manner of extra flavorings – in this case onions. They're wonderful with curries, and the perfect accompaniment for many other dishes. You can buy chapati flour, basically a very fine flour, from an Indian grocer, but otherwise, use half ordinary whole wheat and half all-purpose flour as I have done here. I stick to the authentic method by not adding any salt, but you can add a little if you prefer.

PREPARATION: 15 minutes COOKING TIME: 15 minutes

MAKES 12

1¼ cups (150 g) all-purpose flour, plus extra for dusting

1¼ cups (150 g) fine whole wheat flour

4 scallions, very finely chopped

METHOD

1 Sift the flours into a large bowl and stir in the scallions. Gradually add 1 cup (200 ml) cold water to make a fairly firm dough. Knead vigorously for 5 minutes, then cover with a damp dish towel and set aside to rest.

2 Heat a heavy-based frying pan or griddle, ideally cast-iron, but otherwise non-stick. Divide the dough into 12 balls, dust with flour and roll out into rough 6 inch (15 cm) rounds. Pass the rounds from hand to hand to shake off any excess flour.

3 Cook each chapati in the hot pan for a minute or so on each side until golden and a little puffed. Stack on a plate and keep covered until all the chapatis are cooked, remembering to wipe out the pan with paper towels between each chapati. Serve warm.

CHEF'S TIP: Left-over chapatis can be successfully re-heated in the microwave. Sprinkle a little water on each chapati and re-heat on high power for about 20 seconds or so.

Mozzamary garlic bread

Classic garlic bread with mozzarella cheese and rosemary makes a tasty accompaniment or side dish, but I find it particularly well suited to a bowl of steaming soup, such as the Roasted Tomato and Crème Fraîche Soup on page 42.

PREPARATION: 10 minutes COOKING TIME: 20 minutes

SERVES 4

5 oz (150 g) ball of mozzarella, drained

4 tablespoons (50 g) butter, at room temperature

2 garlic cloves, crushed

2 teaspoons chopped fresh rosemary

¼ teaspoon salt

freshly ground black pepper

1 baguette

METHOD

1 Preheat the oven to 400°F/200°C. Roughly chop the mozzarella, and place in a food processor with the butter, garlic, rosemary, salt and pepper. Whizz together to form a coarse paste.

2 Diagonally slice into the baguette at 1 inch (2.5 cm) intervals, taking care not to slice right through the base.

3 Spread the mozzarella mixture between the slices of bread, smearing any left over across the top.

4 Wrap the loaf in foil, making sure the ends are well sealed, but leaving the top open so that it can crust up in the oven. Bake for 20 minutes until the butter has melted and the cheese is bubbling; serve immediately.

CHEF'S TIP: If the baguette is too long to fit into your oven, just cut into 2 even lengths and wrap individually.

Fern's creamy, crispy onion rings

Now here's a Fern favorite I've prepared many a time on *Ready, Steady, Cook,* as it's easy, goes with so many things and presents beautifully. If you have more time than I did – without Fern asking, 'What's in there?' – soak the onions in milk longer for really creamy, crispy onion rings.

PREPARATION: 5 minutes + soaking time COOKING TIME: 5 minutes

SERVES 2

1 Spanish onion

⅔ cup (150 ml) milk

6 tablespoons seasoned flour

vegetable oil, for frying

METHOD

 Slice the onion into ½ inch (1 cm) wide slices, then separate the rings. Place in a bowl with the milk and set aside for 5–30 minutes (depending on how much time you can spare – the longer the better).

Heat 5 cm (2 inches) of vegetable oil in a deep frying pan.

Drain the onion rings, dust in the seasoned flour, then fry in batches for 2–3 minutes until crisp and golden. Drain on paper towels and eat hot.

Arugula
and roast onion salad

Roasted onions are absolutely delicious. I like to serve them hot as a side vegetable, but they also make an extra-special salad when tossed with peppery arugula and salty parmesan or pecorino.

PREPARATION: 10 minutes COOKING TIME: 30 minutes

SERVES 4

12 pearl onions, halved

3 tablespoons olive oil

sea salt and coarsely ground black pepper

1 tablespoon balsamic vinegar

⅔ cup (50 g) parmesan or pecorino

2 bunches (100 g) arugula leaves

METHOD

1 Preheat the oven to 375°F/190°C. Place the onions in a shallow roasting tin and drizzle over the oil. Season generously and roast for 25–30 minutes until the onions are softened and nicely browned.

2 Drizzle over the balsamic vinegar and allow the onions to cool to room temperature.

3 Using a swivel-style peeler, shave the cheese into wafer-thin slices.

4 Arrange the arugula, roast onions and cheese on 4 serving plates; drizzle round the pan juices and serve.

Arugula and roast onion salad

Pulao rice

Rice makes the perfect accompaniment to many Indian dishes, such as my tasty Lightning Lamb Dhansak (page 86). I've kept my pulao rice quite simple so that it doesn't mask the flavor of the curry you're serving with it.

PREPARATION: 20 minutes COOKING TIME: 25 minutes

SERVES 6

4 tablespoons vegetable oil

3 onions, thinly sliced

1 cinnamon stick

1 teaspoon cumin seeds

3 cardamom pods, cracked

3 star anise

3 cups (500 g) basmati rice, rinsed

2 teaspoons salt

handful cilantro leaves

METHOD

1 Heat the oil in a large pan and cook half the onions over a fairly high heat for about 10 minutes until crisp and lightly browned. Drain on paper towels and set aside, leaving just a coating of oil still in the pan.

2 Add the remaining onions to the pan with the cinnamon, cumin, cardamom, and star anise and cook gently for 5 minutes or so until the onions are golden.

3 Add the rice, cook for 1 minute, then add 3½ cups (1 liter) of cold water and the salt. Bring to a boil, cover and cook over a low heat for 12 minutes until the grains are tender and the water has been absorbed.

4 Remove from the heat and let it stand, covered, for 5 minutes. Transfer to a serving dish and scatter over the fried onions and cilantro leaves; serve warm.

Warm sweet potato
and roast tomato cheese salad

A lovely combination of flavors that works surprisingly well and has instantly become a favorite among friends.

PREPARATION: 15 minutes COOKING TIME: 40 minutes

SERVES 4

3 large (500 g) sweet potatoes, cubed

1 garlic bulb, broken into cloves

3 tablespoons olive oil

1 teaspoon cumin seeds

8 fresh basil leaves, shredded

sea salt and freshly ground black pepper

4 small vines of cherry tomatoes, each with about 5 tomatoes

¾ cup (75 g) strong blue cheese, e.g. Gorgonzola or Stilton

1 tablespoon red wine vinegar

METHOD

1 Preheat the oven to 400°F/200°C. Toss together the sweet potatoes, garlic, 1 tablespoon of the oil, the cumin seeds, basil and some salt and pepper.

2 Arrange on a baking sheet or shallow roasting tin and cook for 25 minutes. Add the tomato vines, trying to keep them intact – if there's not enough room in the tin, place the tomatoes on a separate baking sheet. Drizzle over a little more oil and cook for a further 15 minutes until the tomatoes are softened.

3 Lift off the tomatoes and set aside. Pile the sweet potatoes on to 4 serving plates and scatter over the crumbled blue cheese. Place a tomato vine on top of each and drizzle round a little more oil and a splash of red wine vinegar. Serve warm.

Spicy Spanish patatas bravas

Based on authentic *patatas bravas*, which translates as 'wild potatoes', this dish contains spices that certainly give a fiery flavor, while the cooking aroma gets the juices flowing early. Serve with a bowl of garlic mayonnaise or some of my Lovely Tomato Chutney (page 138).

PREPARATION: 10 minutes COOKING TIME: 40 minutes

SERVES 4

1 lb 2 oz (500 g) baby new potatoes

2 tablespoons olive oil

2 teaspoons paprika

2 teaspoons chili powder

1 teaspoon ground cumin

1 teaspoon sea salt

1 tablespoon finely chopped fresh parsley

METHOD

1 Preheat the oven to 400°F/200°C. Place the potatoes in a strong plastic bag and bash with a rolling pin to crack them. Add the oil, paprika, chili powder, cumin, sea salt, and parsley to the bag, then shake well to mix.

2 Empty the potatoes on to a baking sheet and spread out into a single layer. Roast for 40 minutes, shaking the tray occasionally, until cooked through and nicely browned.

Minted
mashed peas

OK, so you could just open a can – but homemade mushy peas really are terrific (and don't need to be that lurid green). I love to serve them with my Deep-fried Cod in Beer Batter (page 57) and Perfect Golden, Crispy Chips (page 111). Soaking the peas takes a little time, but after that this recipe is really quick, easy and so much cheaper than the canned variety.

PREPARATION: 2 hours COOKING TIME: 20 minutes

SERVES 6

2¼ cups (250 g) quick-soak dried peas

1 teaspoon sea salt

4 tablespoons malt vinegar

1 tablespoon mint sauce

sea salt and freshly ground black pepper

METHOD

1 Soak the peas for 2 hours or according to the packet instructions.

2 Drain the peas and place in a pan with 1½ cups (450 ml) of cold water. Bring to a boil and simmer for 20 minutes until the mixture is tender and thickened.

3 Stir in the salt, vinegar and mint sauce, and season to taste. Serve warm.

CHEF'S TIP: Left-over mushy peas keep very well for a few days, covered, in the refrigerator. Reheat in the microwave.

Hail Caesar salad

The original dressing for this didn't contain anchovies as is commonly thought, so those of you who don't like them needn't miss out. Just sit back and enjoy this classic, which will be around forever. Hail Caesar!

PREPARATION: 15 minutes

SERVES 4-6

1 cos lettuce

6–8 canned anchovies, chopped

1⅓ cups (100 g) Parmesan, grated

FOR THE DRESSING

1 large egg

1 garlic clove, roughly chopped

juice of 1 lime or ½ lemon

2 teaspoons English mustard powder

few shakes of Worcestershire sauce

½ cup (150 ml) olive oil

sea salt and freshly ground black pepper

METHOD

1 Make the dressing: place the egg in a food processor with the garlic, lime or lemon juice, mustard powder, and Worcestershire sauce. With the motor running, slowly pour in the oil to make a smooth sauce about the thickness of light cream. Season to taste and chill until ready to serve.

2 To make a classic caesar salad, tear up the lettuce leaves and mix with the chopped anchovies and grated parmesan. Drizzle with the dressing and scatter over a few Roasted Parmesan Croûtons (page 128).

TRY THIS: The dressing also tastes great drizzled over chicken or large broiled shrimp.

Hail Caesar salad

Roasted parmesan croûtons

These cheesy croûtons are really useful for tossing into bowls of soup and scattering over salads – they add flavor and that all-important crunch. I find that cooking them in the oven gives an even browning and means you can add less oil than when frying them.

PREPARATION: 5 minutes COOKING TIME: 10 minutes

SERVES 2

2 thick slices country style bread

1 tablespoon olive oil

1 tablespoon finely grated parmesan

1 garlic clove, crushed

salt and freshly ground black pepper

METHOD

1 Preheat the oven to 375°F/190°C. Slice the crusts off the bread and discard. Cut the bread into cubes and toss with the olive oil, Parmesan, garlic and salt and pepper. Scatter on to a baking sheet and cook in the oven for 10 minutes until crisp and golden.

2 Allow to cool a little, then serve.

TRY THIS: Ciabatta and flavored focaccia, such as those made with olives or sun-dried tomato, make fantastic croûtons.

New millennium posh potato salad

I like to serve my new potato salad while it's still a little warm, but it's nearly as good after a day in the refrigerator. You can't beat a warm potato salad like this – it's totally comforting, and once on the table, is always the first salad to disappear, so make plenty.

PREPARATION: 15 minutes COOKING TIME: 10 minutes

SERVES 6

1 lb 2 oz (500 g) baby new potatoes, halved

3 oz (75 g) cubed pancetta or lardons

1 garlic clove, crushed

4 anchovies in oil, drained

4 tablespoons mayonnaise

4 scallions, thinly sliced

salt and freshly ground black pepper

METHOD

1 Cook the potatoes in a pan of boiling, salted water for 10 minutes or so, until just tender.

2 Meanwhile, cook the pancetta in a non-stick frying pan for 3–4 minutes until crisp and golden brown; drain on paper towels.

3 Drain the potatoes in a colander and leave to cool a while.

4 Make the dressing: mash together the garlic and anchovies then mix with the mayo. Toss with the warm potatoes, scallions and crispy bacon, season with pepper and serve.

Citrus couscous and golden raisin salad

For a vegetarian treat, you simply can't beat this audacious salad with its wonderful colors, textures, and flavors, which make it absolutely delicious.

PREPARATION: 20 minutes

SERVES 4

1 cup (175 g) couscous

1 cup (300 ml) hot vegetable stock

grated rind and juice of 1 lemon

2 small garlic cloves

6 oz (200 g) carton yogurt

a pinch of sugar

salt and freshly ground black pepper

3 tablespoons olive oil

1 red onion, finely chopped

14 oz (400 g) can chick peas, drained and rinsed

2 tablespoons roughly chopped cilantro, plus sprigs to garnish

⅓ cup (50g) small golden raisins

METHOD

1 Place the couscous in a large ovenproof bowl and pour in the hot stock, then add the lemon rind and juice. Set aside for 10 minutes or so until the liquid has been absorbed.

2 Meanwhile, crush the garlic cloves into the yogurt, add the sugar, and season to taste; set aside.

3 Using a fork, lightly stir the couscous to separate the grains, then gently mix in the olive oil, onion, chick peas, cilantro, and golden raisins. Add salt and pepper to taste. At this stage the salad can be chilled until ready to serve.

4 Divide the salad between 4 side bowls and spoon some of the garlic yogurt on top of each. Lightly ripple it through the top of the salad, then garnish each bowl with a cilantro sprig.

Citrus couscous and golden raisin salad

Maddie's mango chutney

This is a simple chutney with a lovely flavor that develops over time. It's worth the effort of making it yourself as it's so much better than commercially made varieties. Keep it in the refrigerator – I can't tell you how long it will store because it always gets eaten way too quickly in my house. Ask my daughter Maddie…

PREPARATION: 20 minutes COOKING TIME: 40 minutes

MAKES 4 cups (900 ml)

4 garlic cloves, roughly chopped

1 inch (2.5 cm) piece ginger root, coarsely grated

1 red chili, seeded and roughly chopped

½ teaspoon ground turmeric

1 teaspoon cayenne pepper

1½ cups (350 ml) white wine vinegar

2 large green mangoes, cut into ¾ inch (2 cm) cubes

1 teaspoon salt

2 cups (400 g) sugar

4 tablespoons golden raisins

1 star anise

METHOD

1 Place the garlic, ginger, chili, turmeric, cayenne, and a splash of the vinegar in a mini-chopper or food processor and grind to a smooth paste.

2 Put the paste in a large pan with the remaining vinegar, the mangoes, salt, sugar, golden raisins, and star anise. Bring to a boil and simmer for 1 hour or so until the mixture has thickened – don't worry if it stills looks a little watery, as it will thicken further on cooling. Pour into a clean jar, seal, and let it cool. Now, where's that ham sandwich?

Easy mint chutney

If you like a bit on the side, this delicious relish goes with many appetizers, and curries. Try it with Sage and Onion Bhajis (page 8), Celtic Samosas (page 9), and Crispy Crunchy Corn Fritters (page 39). Any left-over chutney can be stirred into plain yogurt and served with poppadums and strips of toasted pita. Or why not make it to go with that take-out curry you've just ordered?

PREPARATION: 5 minutes

SERVES 4

4 mild green chilies, seeded and roughly chopped

1 cup (25 g) fresh mint, chopped

½ cup (15 g) cilantro, chopped

2 teaspoons sugar

1 teaspoon garam masala

½ teaspoon salt

juice of 1 lemon

METHOD

1 Place the chilies, mint, and cilantro in a food processor and whizz until very finely chopped. You might need to stop the processor from time to time and give the mixture a stir.

2 Add the sugar, garam masala, salt, lemon juice, and a tablespoon or two of water. Whizz again until smooth, then chill until ready to serve.

CHEF'S TIP: As always, when using fresh, raw herbs, try not to make this too far ahead of time as the color will fade.

Ainsley's curry sauce to go

It doesn't matter whether you're from Yorkshire or Yarmouth, you can't beat the taste of curry sauce with french fries. When I'm making french fries at home (see page 111), it's too much trouble to go out just for the sauce, so this is my own version and I think it's just like the real thing – gorgeous!

PREPARATION: 10 minutes COOKING TIME: 15 minutes

SERVES 4

1 tablespoon vegetable oil

1 onion, finely chopped

1 red apple, roughly chopped

½ cup (300 ml) vegetable stock

1 tablespoon curry paste

1 tablespoon cornstarch

2 tablespoons frozen peas

2 tablespoons fruity brown sauce

salt and freshly ground black pepper

METHOD

1 Heat the oil in a pan and cook the onion and apple for 3–4 minutes until softened and beginning to brown. Stir in the stock and curry paste and simmer together for 5 minutes.

2 Dissolve the cornstarch in a little water and stir into the sauce with the peas and brown sauce. Bring to a boil and simmer for 2–3 minutes. Season to taste and serve warm (preferably over freshly fried french fries).

TRY THIS: I think the fruity brown sauce is the secret to the success of this recipe, but if you don't have any, try it with regular brown sauce or a tablespoon of chopped sweet pickles.

Real tartare sauce

It's really easy (and a lot nicer) to make your own tartare sauce using shop-bought mayonnaise rather than forking out the premium price charged for a jar of it. Yes, you might have to go out and buy your capers, gherkins and a few other items, but once made, it will keep in the refrigerator for a day or two. Calamari, whitebait and fried fish of any kind all taste great with a spoonful on the side.

PREPARATION: 10 minutes

SERVES 8

6.5 oz (200 g) jar mayonnaise

1 shallot, very finely chopped

2 tablespoons pickled capers, well rinsed and roughly chopped

2 gherkins, roughly chopped

2 teaspoons horseradish sauce

1 teaspoon English mustard

3 tablespoons finely chopped fresh parsley

METHOD

Mix all the ingredients together. Cover and chill until ready to serve.

TRY THIS: Add a squeeze of fresh lemon juice for an extra kick, or a sprinkling of cayenne pepper for an extra, extra kick.

Lovely tomato chutney

This is a really versatile chutney. I love it in a toasted cheese sandwich, on the side with a ploughman's lunch, or dolloped on top of my Wrap and Roll Hot Dogs (page 22). Ooh, lovely!

PREPARATION: 10 minutes COOKING TIME: 60 minutes

MAKES 1 lb 14 oz (850 g)

8 large (1 kg) ripe tomatoes, roughly chopped

1 large onion, chopped

3 garlic cloves, finely chopped

½ cup (150 ml) white wine vinegar

⅞ cup (200 g) light brown sugar

1 teaspoon salt

½ teaspoon dried chili flakes

4 cardamom pods, cracked

¼ teaspoon ground cinnamon

METHOD

1 Place all the ingredients in a large pan. Bring to a boil and simmer for 60 minutes, stirring fairly frequently until thickened and pulpy.

2 Remove from the heat and stir occasionally until cool, then pour into a clean jar, seal, and let it cool completely.

Char-broiled vegetables and hummus ciabatta *with* Lovely tomato chutney

Banana raita

This gorgeous raita is so refreshing and is the perfect accompaniment to curry and spicy dishes. My wife likes to make it just before the take-out arrives.

PREPARATION: 5 minutes

SERVES 2

1 ripe banana

1 garlic clove, crushed

⅔ cup (150g) plain yogurt

juice of ½ lemon

¼ teaspoon salt

METHOD

Mash the banana well with a fork and mix with the garlic and yogurt. Add lemon juice and salt to taste. Serve immediately.

Red onion relish

This relish is particularly nice scattered on top of a green salad, or equally delicious in a tomato cheese sandwich. To toast the cumin seeds, use a dry frying pan set over a medium heat and cook them for 2–3 minutes, stirring all the time.

PREPARATION: 15 minutes

SERVES 4

2 red onions, thinly sliced

½ teaspoon salt

½ teaspoon cumin seeds, toasted

2 tablespoons red wine vinegar

1 red chili, seeded and finely chopped

1 teaspoon sugar

2 tablespoons chopped cilantro

METHOD

1 Place the red onions in a bowl. Sprinkle the salt over them and set aside for 10 minutes.

2 Pat the onions dry and mix with the remaining ingredients. Chill until ready to serve.

Soy dipping sauces

I've got two favorite ways of making this – the first one is a little more fiery than the other. As you get used to the flavors, you can adjust the quantities to suit your taste.

Floating chili soy dipping sauce

For this you need to use an authentic chili oil from an Asian grocer. This contains shrimp paste, so it has more depth than a Mediterranean-style chili oil, which is normally just olive oil and chilies.

PREPARATION: 2 minutes

SERVES 2

4 tablespoons soy sauce

1 teaspoon rice vinegar or white wine vinegar

¼ teaspoon chili oil

pinch of chili flakes (optional)

METHOD

Mix all the ingredients together well and serve. The chili flakes are optional, but look and taste wonderful.

Sweet soy sesame dipping sauce

Preparation: 5 minutes

SERVES 4

3 tablespoons soy sauce

2 tablespoons sake or dry sherry

1 tablespoon brown sugar

½ teaspoon sesame seeds

METHOD

Mix all the ingredients together, stirring until the sugar dissolves.

Sweet chili sauce

I usually make up big batches of this and keep it in the refrigerator because it's so handy for adding to other dishes for a little extra heat and sweetness – and, of course, it's a great accompaniment to all kinds of dishes, such as Celtic Samosas (page 9), Crispy Cache Calamari (page 69), and Pacific Shrimp Fu-yung (page 56).

PREPARATION: 5 minutes COOKING TIME: 5 minutes

SERVES 4

1 tablespoon sunflower oil

1 onion, chopped

2 garlic cloves, finely chopped

2 red chilies, finely chopped

juice of 1 orange

1 tablespoon honey

1 tablespoon malt vinegar

2 tablespoons tomato ketchup

METHOD

1 Heat the oil in a small pan and cook the onion for 2–3 minutes over a medium heat.

2 Add the garlic and chilies and continue to cook for a further 2 minutes, stirring occasionally, until softened.

3 Stir in the orange juice, honey, vinegar, and tomato ketchup and heat through gently until just beginning to bubble. Remove from the heat, cool slightly and serve.

Mama Tahsia's tzatziki

Tzatziki is a Greek classic, so refreshing on the palate, and perfect for jazzing up kebabs, salads, and my recipe for Dimitri's Festive Feta Triangles (page 36).

PREPARATION: 10 minutes

SERVES 4

½ cucumber

¾ cup (200 g) carton yogurt

4 tablespoons chopped fresh mint

2 garlic cloves, crushed

pinch of dried oregano

pinch of sugar

juice of 1 lime

salt and freshly ground black pepper

METHOD

Grate the cucumber into a sieve set over a bowl, or finely dice. (Try to avoid using the central seeded core as it's very watery.) Squeeze out any excess water by presssing the cucumber down into the sieve and transfer to a bowl. Add the yogurt, mint, garlic, oregano, sugar, and lime juice. Season to taste and chill until ready to use.

Portuguese custard tarts

This is one of the best ways I know to finish off a sunny lunch – brilliant with an espresso.

PREPARATION: 20 minutes COOKING TIME: 20 minutes

MAKES 16

⅜ cup (75 g) sugar

2 tablespoons cornstarch

1½ cups (450 ml) milk

2 egg yolks

1 teaspoon vanilla extract

12 oz (375 g) package ready-made puff pastry

flour for rolling

METHOD

1 Place the sugar in a pan with 5 tablespoons of water and gently bring to a boil, stirring until the sugar dissolves.

2 Dissolve the cornstarch in a little of the milk. Whisk the remaining milk, the egg yolks, vanilla extract, and cornstarch mixture into the sugar syrup. Gently bring to a boil, stirring continuously, until smooth and thickened. Cover the custard and allow to cool.

3 Open out the sheet of pastry and roll out a little more to a thickness of ⅛ inch (3 mm). Cut the pastry into 4 inch (10 cm) circles and use them to line a small bun pan (the pastry might come further up the sides of each pan than usual, but it will shrink as it cooks). Refrigerate until the custard is cool.

4 Preheat the oven to 400°F/200°C. Spoon the cooled custard into the tart cases and bake for 20 minutes until the tarts are golden brown. Serve warm or at room temperature.

Iced caffe latte cups

I've taken my favorite milky coffee drink and turned it into a really simple but very stylish ice cream dessert. Make this well ahead of time, but remember to place the cups in the refrigerator for 1 hour or so before serving so that the caffe latte can soften and you won't be in danger of bending your spoons.

PREPARATION: 5 minutes + freezing time

SERVES 6

4 tablespoons sugar

½ cup (100 ml) freshly made espresso coffee

1¾ cups (420 ml) evaporated milk

1 cup (300 ml) light cream

handful roasted coffee beans

cantuccini or chocolate finger cookies , to serve

METHOD

1 Stir the sugar into the coffee until dissolved. Mix in the evaporated milk and cream.

2 Pour into six coffee cups and scatter four or five coffee beans on top of each. Freeze for several hours until frozen solid. About an hour before serving, transfer to the refrigerator, then serve with a biscuit or two on the side.

Rippled raspberry
and white chocolate muffins

I've baked these muffins in waxed paper because it reminds me of breakfasting in continental cafés. Serve with a shot of espresso or a long milky coffee for a luxurious start to the day.

PREPARATION: 20 minutes COOKING TIME: 30 minutes

MAKES 8

2¾ cups (300 g) all-purpose flour

2 teaspoons baking powder

150 g (⅔ cup) sugar

1 egg

1 teaspoon vanilla extract

1 cup (225 ml) milk

4 tablespoons (50 g) butter, melted

½ cup (100 g) fresh raspberries

3 oz (75 g) chopped white chocolate

METHOD

1 Pre-heat the oven to 400°F/200°C. Cut waxed paper into 8 x 6 inch (15 cm) circles and push, creasing the paper to fit, into a muffin pan.

2 Sift the flour and baking powder into a large bowl and stir in the sugar. Crack the egg into a separate bowl and whisk in the vanilla extract, milk, and melted butter.

3 Stir the liquid into the dry ingredients with the raspberries and chocolate, taking care not to over-mix. Spoon the mixture into the paper cases and bake for 30 minutes or so until well risen and just firm.

TRY THIS: Try making these muffins with other fruit, such as blueberries or diced strawberries.

Rippled raspberry and white chocolate muffins

Banana splits
with warm choco-fudge sauce

Remember eating these at your local café? They work best if you've got glass banana-split dishes to serve them in. If you have only upright sundae glasses, cut the bananas into four and push them into the ice cream.

PREPARATION: 10 minutes COOKING TIME: 5 minutes

SERVES 4

FOR THE FUDGE SAUCE

3 tablespoons (150 g) dark chocolate

3 tablespoons (40 g) butter

½ cup (150 ml) heavy cream

½ cup (100 g) dark brown sugar

2 tablespoons corn syrup

FOR THE BANANA SPLITS

4 ripe bananas

12 scoops of ice cream

½ cup (150 ml) heavy cream, lightly whipped

12 glacé cherries

½ cup (50 g) chopped mixed nuts, toasted

8 fan-shaped wafers

METHOD

1 Begin by making the fudge sauce: break the chocolate into a pan and add the butter, cream, sugar, and syrup. Heat gently, stirring, until the ingredients are melted and well blended; remove from the heat, but do not allow to cool completely.

2 Cut each banana in half lengthwise and place in the banana-split dishes, pushing the halves apart. Place 2 scoops of ice cream between 2 pieces of banana.

3 Spoon over the cream, then scatter the cherries on top. Drizzle on the warm sauce, scatter with the nuts, then push in the wafers and serve immediately.

TRY THIS: Traditionally, each split would be topped with one scoop of chocolate ice cream, one of vanilla and one of strawberry – like me, though, you might find it easier to choose just one or two flavors.

Banana splits with warm choco-fudge sauce

Clare's heaven lemon cake

I love a slice of cake with a cup of tea, and this is a really simple one with a deliciously tart lemon flavor. It slices like a dream too. Clare, my wife, came up with the recipe.

PREPARATION: 15 minutes COOKING TIME: 30 minutes

SERVES 8

½ cup + 1 tablespoon (120 g) butter, at room temperature

¾ cup (175 g) sugar

1½ tablespoons grated lemon rind (about 2 lemons)

2 eggs, beaten, at room temperature

½ cup (120 ml) sour cream

½ cup (120 ml) lemon juice (about 2 lemons)

3 cups (350 g) self-rising flour

METHOD

1 Pre-heat the oven to 350°F/180°C. Beat together the butter, sugar, and lemon rind, using an electric whisk, until smooth and light. Beat in the eggs, sour cream, and lemon juice.

2 Sift over the flour and carefully fold in with a metal spoon. Spoon into a greased and lined 8 inch (20 cm) cake pan and bake for 40 minutes until firm and springy to the touch. Allow to cool slightly before transferring to a wire rack.

3 Slice and serve warm with cream as a dessert, or cool completely and serve with a nice cup of tea.

TRY THIS: Make this scrumptious cake a little more child-friendly by topping it with a simple frosting: sweeten 7 oz (200 g) soft cheese with 2 tablespoons of sifted powdered sugar, adding a little milk if the mixture is too stiff.

Clare's heaven lemon cake

Sweet 'n' easy mango lassi

Lassi is a refreshing yogurt-based drink that's often combined with fruit. Mango is the classic fruit used for it (use canned if you can't get fresh), but this recipe also works very well if you substitute a large ripe banana. Whatever the fruit, it's the ideal accompaniment to hot or spicy dishes, as the yogurt cools down the mouth far more efficiently than water.

PREPARATION: 5 minutes

SERVES 2

1 cup (250 ml) plain yogurt

1 cup (150 g) chopped mango flesh

2 tablespoons sugar

METHOD

Blitz all the ingredients together in a blender or food processor. Pour into 2 ice filled glasses and serve.

Fun fresh 'n' healthy juices

Juice bars are springing up all over the place – in fact, juice is the new coffee. If you've invested in an electric juicer, here's a couple of great-tasting, vitamin-packed, healthy drinks for you.

Stripy grape juice

1   Juice the fruit in the order given for a stripy ripple fruit juice.

2   Pass 2 green apples and about 25 white grapes through a juicer and pour into a glass. Now juice about 25 red grapes and pour into the same glass. Drink straight away.

Vegetable patch

Juice 1 ripe tomato, 2 large carrots, and a celery stalk. Pour into an ice filled glass, then add a squeeze of fresh lime juice; stir with a celery stick and serve.

Fresh cherryade

This is nothing like that over-sweet stuff you used to drink bottles of as a kid – no, this is a fragrant drink that's really refreshing and fantastic for picnics and barbecues. Just you watch it disappear.

PREPARATION: 10 minutes + cooling time COOKING TIME: 10 minutes

SERVES 4

2½ cups (400 g) fresh cherries

¼ cup (50 g) sugar

1 sprig fresh tarragon

juice of 2 limes

2 cups (600 ml) soda water

ice and lime twists, to serve

METHOD

1 Place the cherries, sugar and tarragon in a small pan with 1½ cups (450 ml) of water. Gently bring to a boil, stirring until the sugar dissolves, then simmer for 10 minutes until the cherries are very soft.

2 Remove from the heat, then pass through a sieve to remove the stones and tarragon and purée the cherries. Stir in the lime juice, then chill until ready to serve.

3 Transfer to a jug and top up with soda water. Pour into ice filled glasses and serve garnished with lime twists.

Supercallifabulistic soda floats

Here's an old-fashioned Mary Poppins favorite. You can combine the flavors as you wish, but if you're using a fancy ice cream, just serve it with plain soda water, and if you have a fancy fizzy drink, such as a carbonated soda, serve it with plain vanilla ice cream. Of course, you can always throw caution to the wind and try a whole host of wild combinations, but here are a few tried and tasted floats to be getting on with. In each case, place the ice cream in a tall glass, pour over the fizz and serve immediately with straws for sipping. Don't forget the long spoons so you can reach the fizzy ice cream at the bottom of the glass.

EACH FLOAT SERVES 1

Cola float

1 scoop vanilla ice cream

1 cup (250 ml) carbonated soda

Orange soda

1 scoop vanilla ice cream

1 cup (250 ml) orangeade

Chocolate soda

1 scoop chocolate/chocolate chip ice cream

1 cup (250 ml) lemonade

Red berry float

1 scoop raspberry/strawberry ice cream

1 cup (250 ml) limeade

Lemonade and vanilla ice cream float

SWEET BITES & DRINKS | CHAPTER SIX 169

Watermelon smoothie

Pretty similar in fact to a lassi (page 166), smoothies have become increasingly popular as a healthy drink. I've tried many smoothies in my time and this is most definitely my favorite. Like other juice-based drinks, this is really smashing first thing in the morning. An average small watermelon weighs about 7 lb (3 kg), but you don't need to worry too much about the actual weight: just use more or less yogurt to suit your fancy.

SERVES 2

½ small watermelon, about 3¼ lb (1.5 kg), peeled, seeded, and cubed

⅝ cup (150 g) plain yogurt

METHOD

1 Pass the watermelon through a juicer.

2 Place 8 ice cubes in a glass jug and mix with the yogurt; pour in the watermelon juice, mixing well. Pour into glasses and drink immediately.

CHEF'S TIP: I use a juicer but you can whizz the whole thing up in a food processor if you don't have a juicer.

Fresh cherryade *and* Watermelon smoothie

Cardamom-scented
hot chocolate and cream

There are lots of ways to make hot chocolate using cocoa powder or drinking chocolate, but the best flavor comes from melting real milk chocolate into warm milk. If I'm feeling really extravagant, I top each mug with a scoopful of vanilla ice cream or a few marshmallows, followed by the grated chocolate. Total indulgence and a wonderful taste. Go on, get cardamom scented.

PREPARATION: 5 minutes COOKING TIME: 5 minutes

SERVES 4

3½ cups (1 liter) milk

½ teaspoon ground cinnamon

4 cardamom pods, cracked

1½ cups (350 g) milk chocolate

½ cup (100 g) heavy cream

2 tablespoons finely grated semisweet chocolate, to decorate

METHOD

1 Place the milk in a large pan with the cinnamon and cardamom and heat gently. Break the chocolate into the pan and gently bring to a boil, stirring occasionally, until melted.

2 Scoop out the cardamom pods and discard. Pour the hot chocolate into four mugs and top each with a spoonful of extra thick cream; sprinkle over some grated chocolate and serve.

Cardamom-scented hot chocolate and cream *with* Dad's chocolate chip coconut cookies

ACKNOWLEDGMENTS

ONCE AGAIN, AN ENORMOUS AND SPECIAL THANK YOU TO MY FOOD STYLIST AND FRIEND
SYLVANA FRANCO FROM FORK FOR HER CREATIVITY, RECIPE TASTING AND HUMOR. ALSO TO SHARON HEARNE
AND CLARE LEWIS FOR THEIR COMMITMENT AND HARD WORK TASTING AND PREPARING THE DISHES.
IT WAS A REAL TEAM EFFORT. THANKS, GIRLS.

THANKS ALSO TO MY LOCATION CREW: MY SERIES PRODUCER SARA KOZAK, DIRECTOR STUART BATEUP,
ASSISTANT PRODUCER VICKY JEPSON, RESEARCHER MELANIE STANLEY, PRODUCTION ASSISTANT JENNY WRIGHT,
CAMERAMAN ALAN DUXBURY, SOUND RECORDIST ANDY MORTON AND EDITOR KEITH BROWN.

I'D ALSO LIKE TO THANK BBC TELEVISION AND BBC BOOKS, ESPECIALLY MY COMMISSIONING EDITOR
NICKY COPELAND, PROJECT EDITOR RACHEL BROWN AND DESIGNER JOHN CALVERT, CRAIG EASTON AND
GUS FILGATE FOR BEAUTIFUL PHOTOGRAPHY, ELROY THOMAS FOR STANDING IN, MY AGENTS JEREMY HICKS
AND SARAH DALKIN, AND LAST BUT NOT LEAST MY LOVELY WIFE CLARE AND OUR VERY SPECIAL CHILDREN,
JIMMY AND MADELEINE...AND MY PET DOG OSCAR POSKA.